THE REMAKING OF CHRISTIAN DOCTRINE

Maurice Wiles

THE REMAKING OF CHRISTIAN DOCTRINE

The Hulsean Lectures 1973

SCM PRESS LTD

334 01423 9

First published 1974
by SCM Press Ltd
56 Bloomsbury Street, London
Second impression 1975

© SCM Press Ltd 1974

Printed in Great Britain by
Billing & Sons Ltd
Guildford and London

CONTENTS

PREFACE

This book embodies the Hulsean lectures given at Cambridge in the Michaelmas Term, 1973. They are printed here very much in the form in which they were delivered. I have added as an appendix a separate paper on 'The Resurrection of the Body'. This was not one of the lectures, but was written at the same time and develops the same approach in relation to a more specific item of Christian belief. It was also first delivered in Cambridge as a paper to the Cambridge Theological Society. I am grateful to my old university for the stimulus provided by these invitations and the discussions to which they gave rise.

1

INTRODUCTION: THE PRESENT TASK OF DOCTRINE AND ITS RELATION TO THE PAST

A few years ago I published a small book entitled *The Making of Christian Doctrine*. The title was intended to convey a double meaning. The aim of the book was twofold. On the one hand its concern was historical; it was an attempt to understand more fully some of the ways by which the church of the patristic age first came to formulate her faith in a comparatively systematic form. In that respect it was a study of the initial (and therefore unrepeatable) 'making' or formation of Christian doctrine. But the book had a normative or methodological concern as well; it was an attempt at the same time to reflect upon that historical process in a way which would throw some light on the continuing task of Christian doctrinal work. In that respect it was a study of the way in which Christian doctrine is always in the making, in the process of formation.

In this book I shall be aiming to apply the insights gained from those earlier reflections more directly to the work of contemporary Christian doctrine. In order to give expression to the close connection, in my own mind at least, between the two enterprises, I have given it the title of *The Remaking of Christian Doctrine*. I have done so with some hesitation. For it runs the risk of giving a seriously misleading impression.

It could easily be taken to imply the notion that I was hoping to provide here a once-for-all revision of the church's initial doctrinal achievement. Nothing could be further from my mind. 'Remaking' is not intended to suggest any such once-for-all reformation of Christian doctrine. It is designed rather to stress the continually changing and essentially temporary nature of the doctrinal task as I understand it. Our concern in doctrine is with what has to be said here and now; and we should be as unwilling for whatever we may decide we have to say to be binding on the future as we are ourselves unwilling to be bound by the past. Sufficient unto the day are the problems thereof.

But an unwillingness to be bound by the past does not necessarily involve a total disregard of it, and in the case of Christian doctrine it certainly should not do so. The relation between Christian doctrine today and its earlier manifestations is usually spoken of in terms of development. In *The Making of Christian Doctrine* I argued that the concept of development needs to be understood in a very loose and open way. Two reviewers of that book have claimed that the position maintained in it constitutes in effect a dissolution of the idea of development altogether; that whereas I had set out to write about the development of doctrine, I had in fact abolished the notion altogether without realizing that I had done so. My main concern here will be, as I have said, with doctrinal activity as it is being and should be carried on today. But our attitude to the doctrinal formulations of the past is so integral a part of that activity that some consideration of the question raised by the two reviews is called for by way of introduction.

Robert Wilken, writing in the *Journal of Religion*, says:

The notion of a development of doctrine is a sophisticated way of expressing the patristic notion that there was a body of beliefs handed over to the apostles by Jesus and that these beliefs form the substance of Christian faith. Most theologians would, of course, deny this claim of the fathers, but to speak of development inevitably raises the question of whether a development is legitimate or illegitimate, and the basis for judging legitimacy will be some historical point in the past, as, for example, the apostolic age. Thus it is interesting that by the end of his book Wiles has really given up the question of legitimacy and illegitimacy of doctrinal developments. Instead, he speaks of a continuity based on certain activities which define and identify the Christian community: expounding the Scriptures, worship, the experience of salvation. By any standard, it is difficult to see how those three activities can provide rational and cognitive norms for Christian thinking. Exegesis, worship, and the experience of salvation are as diverse as the Christian theological tradition. But it is indisputable that they profoundly inform and influence Christian thought. The drift of Wiles's answer suggests that the older problem of doctrinal development is really a dead issue and was perhaps a false problem to begin with. Wiles does not say this, but, by the end of the book, the problem seems to have been dissolved. And this is good.[1]

Robert Evans makes a similar point when he concludes his review in the *Journal of the American Academy of Religion* with these words:

The question which he does not face directly is whether the category of development is really useful either in the analysis of Christian historical materials or in his program for contemporary theological statement. Newman's word suggests a process of organic unfolding which cannot help but be misleading in characterizing the sort of fresh start *with identity of aims* which the author is commending, nor does the term help much in suggesting the character of that often painful and tortuous process of assimilation of old to new which Wiles so well describes within the patristic period itself. If the term is retained, it means little more than 'history'—the history of novel attempts to state the intellectual content of Christian

[1] Robert Wilken, Review of *The Making of Christian Doctrine*, *Journal of Religion* 49, 1969, p.313.

faith relative to pressures and backgrounds which are continually shifting.[2]

Everything has a history. Not everything is appropriately described as a 'development' of that which has gone before it. It is not easy to determine where the word is or is not appropriate. The connotation of the term varies for different people. The only way to assess its appropriateness is by considering the kind of implication that it has been or could properly be understood to bear. In what ways has or can the relation of contemporary doctrine to its earlier formulations be conceived?

In the first place it can be (and certainly has been in the past) claimed that the relation is essentially one of identity. The varying doctrinal utterances of the church at different points in her history certainly do not appear to be identical; but it could be claimed that apparent innovation is not real innovation, but only the drawing out of what is already implicit in the earliest formulations. The natural analogy would be that of a deductive argument. Contemporary doctrine would be like the conclusion of a deductive argument, which in one sense is already fully contained in the premises and which can claim novelty only in the sense that it had not been explicitly seen to be the case before the actual deduction had been made. But however respectable a place such a view may have in Christian history, it would be so little maintained today and seems to me to be so self-evidently false that I do not propose to spend any time in discussion of it here.

A second approach is one which the word 'development' most naturally suggests—namely the analogy of growth.

[2] Robert Evans, Review of *The Making of Christian Doctrine, Journal of the American Academy of Religion*, Vol. XXXVIII, No. 1, 1970, pp.111f.

The attractiveness of this model has been that it seems to provide a picture which allows for novelty without innovation, one which can do justice to the reality of change in a way the logical theory cannot, but which still preserves a strong sense of identity with the point of origin. The flower is not contained in the seed in the same way as the conclusion of a deductive argument is contained in the premises, but it can be spoken of in very similar terms as already there latent within the seed. This means that the model can appeal both to those who want to stress unchanging identity at the core and to those who want to stress genuine innovation. The former (though they would not relish the comparison) are a bit like those reductionists who in the face of the evolution of the human species want to say that man is really nothing but his animal ancestry in another form; the latter by contrast would be comparable to those who speak of emergent or creative evolution.

If that comparison is allowed to stand, then this form of the development model would seem to be quite heavily weighted in the direction of stress on innovation. But a distinction needs to be made. Those who have spoken of development have for the most part not wanted it to be understood in terms of evolution generally, but rather in terms of development controlled by the inherent nature of the developing object itself. Thus Blondel distinguishes what is 'only *evolution*, that is to say the effect of external pressures or of interdependent influences, from what is vital development, that is to say continuous creation starting from a germ which transubstantiates its own nourishment'.[3] Clearly any such distinction must be less than

[3] M. Blondel, *The Letter on Apologetics, and History and Dogma,* Harvill Press 1964, pp.255f., cited by J. P. Jossua, 'Progrès ou structurations des doctrines?', *Revue des Sciences Philosophiques et Théologiques* 52, 1968, p.196.

absolute. For nothing develops in total independence of its environment. But in relation to Christian doctrine the distinction has to face a further difficulty. We only know what is latent in the seed because we have a host of specimens which we have been able to observe. It is on this basis that we are, for example, able to identify some growths as malformations. But there is only one Christian history. The concept of development as such does not therefore provide any criteria for distinguishing between true and false developments, as critics of Newman's essay are never tired of pointing out.[4] The most the model can do in this respect is to encourage us to look for a germinal expression of doctrine at the outset of the life of the church, incorporating within itself clear indications of the proper lines of its own desired development. It is precisely because he regards such a search as a hopelessly false trail that Wilken believes the concept of development to be an unhelpful and undesirable one.

The approach to the problem which I used in my earlier book was a comparison between the development of doctrine and the development of other branches of human knowledge, such as science, history and so forth. This still seems to me to be a valuable approach. One does not need to claim that the development of doctrine must be identical with that of other areas of intellectual knowledge—they do not, indeed, all develop in the same way as one another; one need only claim that the comparison may prove fruitful

[4] Nicholas Lash, *Change in Focus,* Sheed and Ward 1973, p.97, argues that it was not Newman's aim to provide such criteria. If so, many of the criticisms often raised against the essay would fall to the ground, but only at the cost of drastically reducing the usefulness and applicability of the book's approach outside its own very specific and personal terms of reference.

and illuminating. Now what strikes me as the most significant feature in the development of intellectual disciplines is that the most important changes occur when somebody succeeds in seeing the subject from a new perspective. It is a new frame of reference rather than new particular facts (though the former is often set off by the latter) which is most productive of advance. Now when you see something from a new perspective, everything is altered. The element of identity that persists through a change of that kind is not to be sought in any key set of particulars which remain totally unaltered; rather it is to be found in a continuing similarity of shape or character which is compatible with some change in every particular. To take a simple visual example: if one looks at a human face from a new angle, it may look very different, and yet one may at the same time be able confidently to identify it as the same face. That will not be because any one feature, say the eyes or the nose, has been unaffected by the change; even if it is the eyes or the nose that provide the clue which helps to convince us that it is the same face, it will not be because they appear just the same from the new perspective, but will rather be due to the way in which they draw attention to the distinctive cast or character of the face as a whole.

Here, then, is another model for conceiving the changing pattern of doctrinal belief. One might call it change through alteration of perspective. Differing cultural and philosophical conditions require different understandings and articulation of the Christian faith. The element of identity will be much more difficult to define. It will have to be looked for in the sources to which reference is made, the kinds of concern which direct that reference and the general pattern or character of the affirmations made. Wilken argues that this kind of an approach ought not to be called 'development' at all, because it does away with the concept of an initial given seed which unfolds into the full flower of Christian doctrine. This seems to me to restrict the implication of the word somewhat too narrowly. The word 'development' is, in fact, used in a very wide variety of ways. But if it is likely to be misleading, by all means let it go.

Similar misgivings about the term 'development' are also being voiced by some Roman Catholic scholars today. J. P. Jossua, for example, in an interesting article finds Moehler's conception of homogeneous development over-optimistic, not to say triumphalist, in character; it cannot do justice to the vagaries of the tradition as it is seen to be, in which one has to acknowledge of different encyclicals, for example, that even if they do not formally contradict one another, yet 'l'on dit tout autre chose sur le même subjet'. To speak of development in the singular rather than developments in the plural seems to Jossua to be a hangover from the 'fixisme' of bygone ages.[5]

But the appropriateness or otherwise of the word 'development' is not the main issue. The important question is to decide whether this third model is one which helps us to understand accurately the facts of the case. It seems to me that it certainly is appropriate in helping us to see the way in which Christian truth has been and needs to be expressed in terms of differing philosophies and differing cultural traditions. No one today, it is true, is likely to deny that as a statement at the theoretical level. But few of us have yet taken in at the deeper levels of consciousness the fluidity in doctrine which such an acknowledgement is bound to entail. In so far as my third model helps to bring this truth home at the level of the general imagination, it

[5] J. P. Jossua, art. cit., pp.194–7. See also Nicholas Lash, *Change in Focus*, pp.148f.

is fulfilling a vitally important role of precisely the kind that a good model is designed to fulfil.

But I have freely to admit that it does not give us much help with regard to the problem of the relation of contemporary doctrine to its origins. Science, art and philosophy are all concerned with aspects of experience in general; they do not have the kind of relationship to their own past that Christianity has been understood to have. Nor do I think that Christian doctrine has been wrong in recognizing something special about its relationship to its own past, to the events of Christ's life and the scriptural witness to them in particular. The various accounts that it has given of the special nature of that relationship may all turn out to be highly unsatisfactory in one way or another. This is an area of thought in which considerable change in an age of changing historical consciousness is only to be expected. But however great those changes may prove to be, I do not envisage that they will involve doing away with the sense of a special relationship to the past altogether. And in that case the help that this third model can give us remains strictly limited. Even if against Wilken I prefer to hold on to the term development, I have to agree with him on the main point; I am bound to concede that the conception does not help us at precisely the point it has been thought to be of help, namely a clarifying of the relation between our doctrinal statements today and those of the earliest stage of Christian history. Is there any other approach to the problem which will take us further?

We can attempt to approach the question in a way which seeks its inspiration not so much from analogy with other disciplines but more directly from within the heart of Christian theology itself. The farewell discourses of the Fourth Gospel ascribe to Jesus the words: 'I have yet many things to say unto you but you cannot bear them now. 'Howbeit when he, the Spirit of truth, is come, he will guide you into all truth' (John 16.12f.). The text is one that has been much used in the past by those who wanted biblical foundation for the conviction that all true knowledge in art or science is God-given. This, it would be generally agreed, is not what the text is saying. The text must be understood in relation to the Fourth Gospel's understanding of 'truth', and in particular to the claim of Jesus earlier in the discourses to be the truth. Its primary intention is certainly to insist that Jesus embodies the truth in himself as a person, that his full significance was not grasped by his disciples during his lifetime, but that it will be disclosed by the Spirit in the life of the church. It thereby reminds us that the problem of development is intimately related to the problem of christology. It is if and when we think of the problem of development simply as the problem of how to relate contemporary doctrine to earlier doctrinal formulations that Wilken's challenge is most unanswerable. Early doctrine was never a simple, coherent statement of faith which can be conceived as the compact seed from which all subsequent doctrine is an organic growth. If that were the only thing that could be meant by speaking of development in this context, then no fault could be found with his conclusion that 'the older problem of doctrinal development is really a dead issue and was perhaps a false problem to begin with'. Is there any escape from this conclusion if we pose the problem in a more christological form, as the Fourth Gospel text suggests? A number of scholars have attempted to do this. De Lubac, for example, has written: 'Le point de depart et le substance même du dogme est moins un enseignement qu'une personne.'[6] This certainly appears at first sight to offer a promising approach. It sounds religiously impressive and positive. It preserves the church's christological confession in a strong form. It provides another helpful model of how truth may be implicit at one stage (i.e. in the mind or being of a person), and may become explicit later as the mind of that person finds adequate expression, and as what he is in himself is progressively grasped by others. But what exactly does the assertion imply? Can we spell out what it really means?

It seems to me to be capable of a wide range of possible meanings. Let me try to illustrate this by spelling out two possible meanings at different ends of the scale. At one end of the scale the statement becomes a kind of tautology. Jesus is affirmed to be the incarnation of the divine Logos, the earthly embodiment of the very mind and wisdom of God, who is of one substance with the Father. Therefore all truth (and *a fortiori* all truth about God) must by definition be in him. It may not have been expressed by Jesus of Nazareth; may not indeed have been consciously present to his mind or even available to his consciousness (however that would be determined), but that is irrelevant and can be dealt with by a kenotic theory of incarnation or some similar means. It would still be true that all doctrinal truth would be an unfolding of that which was present among us in the person of the incarnate Logos. At the other end of the scale it could be argued that no truth can be claimed as a proper element in Christian doctrine unless it can be linked to the person of the historic Jesus either as what he explicitly taught or as what is implied by his life and ministry as witnessed to in the gospels and by the earliest preaching about him. But this approach soon runs into difficulties. It is questionable how far we can know what was explicitly

⁶ H. de Lubac, 'Le problème du développement du dogme', *Recherches de Science Religieuse* XXXV, 1948, p.158 (echoing Lebreton).

taught by Jesus; in so far as we can, it was taught within a first-century setting and needs translation before it can be incorporated into contemporary doctrine. 'What is implied by his life and ministry' is an impossibly wide concept. It is true that the so-called 'kerygma' has been claimed by some to provide a basic datum of just this kind. But to me that 'kerygma' appears to be one particular form of interpretation of the New Testament, conditioned like all others by the particular circumstances in which it arose, rather than something which emerges inescapably as of timeless and changeless character from the records themselves.

Wilken argued that the strength of the development concept was that (if valid) it provided some point in the historic past by reference to which the legitimacy of subsequent developments might be tested. But if we think of the starting point as a person (which appeared to be the most attractive form of the development concept), it can hardly be made to serve this purpose. In my first form—the Alexandrian approach, if I may use that term very loosely —it is clearly no test at all; what is believed on other grounds to be true is thereby believed to have been implicit in the person of the incarnate Logos, rather than the other way round. In my second form, with its greater emphasis on history, the norm is either inaccessible or too narrow—and probably both. It does not seem as if in practice we are saying more than that in seeking to assess the truth of any Christian doctrine one ought to relate it to the person of Christ and the scriptural witness to him—and in that attenuated form it is no more than a statement of something that would be common ground to every conceivable purveyor of Christian doctrine whatever. Our christological test turns out to be very much weaker than had appeared likely at first.

But the Johannine text from which we began this discussion is not wholly or even primarily christological in character. If Christ is the truth into which the disciples are to be led, it is the Spirit that will lead them there.

Our inability to cope with the problem of development in exclusively christological terms should not surprise us. The early church is often accused of being binitarian in its theology, but the very early church, at least, was in many ways more trinitarian in its practice than we are. It took the leading of the Holy Spirit very seriously. By itself the concept of the leading of the Spirit does not take us any further in our concern to determine the legitimacy or otherwise of proposed doctrinal developments. For the concept of the Spirit's guidance *by itself* can be used to legitimate anything, which means that it can be used to legitimate nothing. But then the idea of the Spirit's guidance *by itself* is not a genuinely Christian notion. The context of the Johannine text reminds us that the Spirit is the Spirit of Christ: 'He will not speak on his own authority ... he will take what is mine and declare it to you.' What, then, is the significance of adding to the concept of Jesus who embodies the truth the further concept of the Spirit who leads us into that truth? Surely this. The Spirit is the wind which blows where it wills, who is sovereign and free in relation to man. If it is he who leads us into the truth of Jesus, then we need to recognize that while our attempts to discover true doctrine must always be related to Jesus, there cannot be any external tests by which we can know if we are doing the job rightly or not. If that is what is implied by the desire to find ways of legitimating our doctrinal affirmations, the sooner we abandon the search for such ways the better. We have to go on with the hermeneutical task, trying to understand as fully as we can the scriptural witness to Jesus; we have to go on seeking to respond to God through him in prayer and worship. On the basis of all that, Christians have to try to say what seems to them to be true about God and his dealings with the world. We will certainly be limited, and may well be wrong, even in what seems to us as individuals most clearly to be true; we will certainly be limited, and we may well be wrong, even in what seems to us as a formal gathering of the church or of the churches most clearly to be true. The Spirit is sovereign and does not guarantee to underwrite even our most faithful and devoted undertakings. But if we are working in the way I have outlined, and if we take seriously our own limitations and our own fallibility, we must then affirm what seems to us to be true. We have to take our stand there; we can do no other.[7]

We are thus brought back once again to the position that we cannot lay down any rules about the relation of contemporary doctrine to the affirmations of the past which will not be so general as to offer no practical guidance at all. We cannot provide in advance a blueprint of how doctrine is to be done.[8] Indeed, it was perhaps somewhat absurdly naïve to suggest that such a thing could conceivably be possible. As with other fields of study, the most that we can hope to do is to point to some of the principles which must be borne in mind in any approach to the subject in question.

[7] This position is very close to that described by Jaroslav Pelikan as a 'confessional' position in relation to doctrinal truth, which seeks to go beyond the antithesis of historical relativism and the claim to absolute truth (Jaroslav Pelikan, *Historical Theology: Continuity and Change in Christian Doctrine*, Philadelphia: Westminster Press 1971, p.159).

[8] Cf. Karl Rahner, 'Pluralism in Theology and the Unity of the Church's Profession of Faith', *Concilium* 6, 5, 1969, p.55. 'We certainly cannot set down *a priori* norms that would tell us automatically when a theology is using its new found responsibility correctly and when the magisterium has to step in to challenge heterodoxy.'

In the case of doctrine we can recall the importance of attention to the biblical sources, to the history of the church and to contemporary experience; we can stress that it is not an exclusively intellectual affair, but has intimate connections with worship and ethics. It would be possible to attempt to refine these principles and give them more precise expression. But it is questionable how far such a procedure could take us. The most creative work in any discipline is never the outcome of simply applying the principles of that study by rote. And any advance even in our understanding of such principles themselves most commonly arises by retrospective reflection on the way in which creative exponents of that skill have in fact worked. So we may hope to make most progress if we attempt to do the job itself—but to do it in a consciously self-critical manner. In these lectures, therefore, I intend to explore the central area of Christian doctrine—our understanding of God and his relation to the world in the spheres of creation, redemption and grace. I shall leave on one side further direct discussion of the problems of theological method, not in the belief that they have been solved and that the doctrinal task can now be undertaken with confidence about how one ought to proceed, but rather in the hope of learning by experiment something more about the proper execution of the task. I shall not, of course, in the compass of a single short course of lectures be able to explore that area very deeply, but I hope to be able to do it in a way which will throw light on the proper nature of doctrinal work as a whole.

There is, however, one other preliminary issue that calls for discussion before we leave questions of method and embark on the substantive issues themselves. I have been talking about some of the problems involved in undertaking the work of Christian doctrine today. I have simply assumed that the task is going to be undertaken. But why should it be undertaken? What is doctrine for? What role is it intended to fulfil?

Academic practitioners are often regarded as almost neurotically introspective and self-critical. Yet they do not in practice reflect overmuch on the purpose and objectives of their particular activities. The literary critic, for example, lectures and writes about the great figures of the past. But what is his purpose in so doing? Is he seeking to persuade other people that his way of understanding those writers is the true one, and so get them to adopt it also? Or is it perhaps part of a personal struggle on his own part to understand those writers, a struggle in which he is inviting others to share as much in the hope of receiving enlightenment as of providing it? Or is he really more concerned to heighten the general sensibilities of those to whom he lectures in their response to the world around them, and to use the figures from the past more as an aid to that objective than from any intrinsic concern with the precise historical interpretation of the writers themselves? No doubt all are legitimate aims, and in most cases all will be present in some degree or another; but misundertanding would sometimes be avoided if both lecturer and audience were clearer which aim was uppermost at any particular moment.

Religious talk is an even more luxuriant growth than literary talk. It serves many varied purposes: preaching, prayer, meditation. Theology or doctrine is one form of such talk, but it too can have very diverse purposes. It may be concerned primarily with proclamation of the faith as accepted by the main body of the church, or with the answering of particular questions and difficulties that have been raised by critics of the faith, or again with the clarification of the theologian's own mind. The form that it takes will in part be determined by the particular purpose envisaged, and will not be identical in all cases.

What, then, is the particular purpose of the Christian doctrine that I shall be seeking to discuss and to develop in these lectures? The two words that best describe my objectives are 'coherence' and 'economy'. They are not perhaps the most obvious or the most immediately attractive objectives for the doctrinal theologian to set before him. An unfriendly critic might describe them as euphemisms for 'rationalism' and 'reductionism'. Nevertheless, I believe them to be important aims. Like everything else in life they can be abused and misapplied. But *abusus non tollit usum*; the risk of abuse calls not for their abandonment but rather for a more careful statement of the precise nature of the use intended.

Within the rich field of Christian doctrine as a whole, different themes may be taken up on different occasions and each may properly be developed in relative independence of the other. We do not need to be concerned all the time about the way in which one area of discourse relates to all the others. But 'coherence' remains an important goal. We do need to check whether the different affirmations that we are led to make at various times and for various purposes are consistent with one another. A concern for 'coherence' only becomes objectionable and deserving of the opprobrious title of 'rationalism' if the criteria of consistency are regarded as fixed in advance and rigidly applied without adequate sensitivity to the particular nature of the subject matter involved.

Similarly, there are occasions on which an imaginative expansiveness is the most appropriate path to follow in seeking to give expression to religious realities. But such imaginative expansiveness requires the doctrinal theologian's concern for 'economy' as a kind of dialectical partner in the attempt of the church as a whole to find the most adequate expression of the truth. The tradition in which we live does not stand still. It is constantly changing, and we have a role to play in guiding the direction that those changes shall take. One important contribution to the fulfilling of that role lies in drawing distinctions between what the evidence requires us to say and what the evidence does not disallow us from saying. It is an insistence on distinguishing what the evidence requires us to say that I have in mind in speaking of the objective of 'economy'. There are analogies here with traditional distinctions between dogma and theology, or with the limited negative and corrective role customarily ascribed to conciliar decisions. In those cases also there was an attempt to delineate what was essential, and to distinguish it not only from what was false but also from what were to be regarded as no more than possible theological constructions—allowable but not required. Such analogies must not be pressed too far. The distinctions that we may feel able to make will certainly not be endowed with the same unchanging or exclusive character that has usually marked such activity in the past. Even where accepted as valid, such distinctions will not be valid for all people or for all time. They will be valid in relation to the evidence now available to us, as understood from within a broad but necessarily specific and limited tradition. To stress this objective may appear to be to ascribe to the work of doctrine a somewhat astringent role. It may indeed involve the pruning of some luxuriant growths that have come to be highly valued. But pruning is not only not destructive; it is a necessary contribution to any healthy future growth.

A careful concern for 'coherence' and 'economy' are not the only objectives a theologian might properly set before him. But they do seem to be to be essential ingredients in any worthwhile approach towards the remaking of Christian doctrine. It is, therefore, with these objectives in view, that I propose to discuss in the next four chapters the Christian understanding of God, of Christ, of atonement, and finally of grace and the Holy Spirit. In the final chapter I shall make some attempt to draw together the discussion and to reflect on the kind of doctrinal pattern to which it points.

2

GOD

'Death of God theology' has proved itself a notoriously elusive as well as a deservedly evanescent concept. If it was intended to declare either that there never had been or that there was not now any transcendent reality as a referent for the word 'God', then it would have been better entitled 'the death of God and of theology'. If on the other hand it was intended to affirm either that some conceptions of God commonly held in the past had now to be abandoned or that there were particular difficulties in affirming the reality of God at the present time, it was saying something both true and important, but seeking a spurious kind of attention by saying it in a misleadingly sensational manner. *The Problem of God Today* (to quote the title of a recent lecture by John Macquarrie[1]) or even *God the Problem* (to quote the title of a book by that much underrated theologian, Gordon Kaufman[2]) would have been fairer designations of the position, though they in their turn could be challenged as failing to do full justice to the stringency of the situation to which death of God language was intended to draw attention. Perhaps the character of the situation is best

[1] John Macquarrie, *The Problem of God Today*, Drawbridge Memorial Lecture, Christian Evidence Society 1972.

[2] Gordon Kaufman, *God the Problem*, Harvard University Press 1972.

represented by the title of yet another, slightly earlier, book—*The Eclipse of God*.[3]

For it is important to realize that the problem goes deeper than simply the question of the grounds on which it is possible for us to affirm belief in God, as if it were simply a matter of acknowledging that there may need to be a change of route by which belief in God can most properly be established at the present time. The epistemological problem has more wide-ranging consequences than that way of putting it implies. How knowledge of God is accessible to us affects not only the way in which such knowledge comes to us; it also affects the way in which it has to be expressed. And it affects not only the way in which that knowledge is to be expressed; it affects also the proper content of that knowledge.

Ever since the time of Kant, theologians have been acutely aware of the extreme difficulty of reasoning from experience of the world to affirmation about a transcendent God. To some it has appeared to be not a question of difficulty but of impossibility. Some totally different mode of apprehension was felt to be needed if affirmation about God were to have a sound basis. Two such other approaches have played a prominent part in recent theology, and the differences of approach have involved substantial differences in the content of doctrine.

This is not the place to undertake a detailed examination of the theology of the last two centuries. That task has frequently been essayed and will continue to be so. It is one that needs to be done and to be redone, for without such careful critical scrutiny of our immediate forebears we are

[3] Martin Buber, *The Eclipse of God*, Gollancz 1953. It is used by T. F. Torrance as the title of a chapter in *God and Rationality*, Oxford University Press 1971.

unlikely to find the right way forward for ourselves. But here I want to venture simply an impressionistic sketch in the hope that it may throw some light on what the general pattern and shape of that way forward will need to be.

If one rejects the possibility of arguing from premises about the world to conclusions about God but is still convinced that theology is a proper and necessary activity, what ways of proceeding are open? Two contrasting moves are possible. Some change will have to be made in respect either of the premise or of the conclusion. The first possible move, then, is to reject the premise, to deny that experience of the world is the appropriate starting-point for theology. To regard it as such, it may be argued, is not only philosophically untenable but religiously unacceptable also. God is wholly other, he is not a bit of our world, not within our measure; there is an infinite qualitative difference between him and us. To believe that we can start from a knowledge of the world and end up with a knowledge of God is therefore both an invalid *metabasis eis allo genos* and the grossest impiety. God is not an object about whom we make discoveries; if we are to know him at all, it can only be because he is a subject who freely chooses to make himself known to us. And God, it is claimed, has so chosen to reveal himself in Jesus Christ and in his Word. Moreover, since it would be self-contradictory to claim that God has revealed himself, yet given no valid knowledge of himself, it follows that here (but here alone) a real and rational knowledge of God is available to us. Without detriment to the transcendent otherness of God, we can speak intelligibly and truly about him simply and solely because that knowledge and the appropriate language to express it are given us in revelation.

There is no questioning the religious impressiveness of this conception. It impresses by its combination of logical coherence and religious vigour. It impresses the more when developed and worked out with the majestic power of Barth's mind and pen. But conceptions, however impressive have to be tested against the facts. It seems unmistakably clear to me that we simply do not have the kind of explicit self-revelation that such a scheme requires. When everything has been said about the eyes of faith which are enabled by God to grasp the Word within the words, the claim that in Christ and in the Word by which he is made known to us we have a revelation of this distinctively different kind still seems to me to be a judgment both arbitrary and indefensible. However revelation is to be understood, the medium through which it comes to us is so much a part of our ordinary world that we have to assess it, to judge it, to evaluate it—and at once all the problems of starting from our finite knowledge of this finite world which it was intended to bypass come flooding back inescapably.

Countless words have been written by people in the position in which I find myself—powerfully impressed by the greatness of Barth and of his work, yet totally unable to accept the fundamental premises upon which his whole theological enterprise rests. I do not intend to add to them. I wish only to quote some words which sum up my response to his work better than any others I have come across—and they are words not written about Barth or even about a theologian at all. They are the reaction of a historian, W. H. Walsh, to the work of Arnold Toynbee, but only the names of the person and of the discipline need to be changed to give precise expression to what I would want to say about Barth.

We seem to have to do with a personal vision rather than a scientific hypothesis, with the deliverances of a poet or a 'philosopher-hierophant' (Toynbee's own description of Spengler) rather than a sober investigator with both feet on the ground. And the impression is confirmed when we observe the remarkable twist given to the *Study* in the last four volumes, where interest is shifted from establishing laws of history to discovering the meaning of history as a whole, and where the intensely personal character of the whole enterprise is distressingly evident. The delusion that these last volumes are contributions to history is so easy to avoid it is astonishing that it should continue to blind Toynbee himself.

What then are we to do about Toynbee? The answer is read him, but read him as one might read a poet or a metaphysician, to see whether his way of looking at the past carries conviction or the reverse. At the lowest estimate this procedure will lead, in a writer of such breadth of knowledge and sweep of vision, to a diminution of parochialism and perhaps the seeing of hitherto unsuspected connections; at the best it could produce in a sympathetic reader an understanding of the historical process as a whole such as he has derived from no previous writer. But I confess that reading Toynbee has not had this effect in my own case.[4]

Barth, then, is to be read (some of him, at least), but not to be imitated. Whatever there is to be learnt from him (and like Walsh I gladly recognize that for some that will be a great deal more than in my own case), I am convinced that his basic approach is not one that points us the way forward. There can be no rejection of the premise. We have no other starting-point than our ordinary experience of the world. We must turn, therefore, to the second possible move of which I spoke. If the premise is to stand, it is the conclusion which must call for rejection, or at least for modification. Perhaps theology must after all abandon its claim to speak about the transcendent God; not in the paradoxical sense of becoming an atheistic theology, but in the sense that it will speak only of the effects of God as experienced, and make no attempt to speak of God in himself. It may be

[4] W. H. Walsh, 'Meaning in History', in P. Gardiner (ed.), *Theories of History*, Allen and Unwin 1960, pp.306f.

that theology is rightly to be defined in Bultmann's words as 'the conceptual account of the existence of man as being determined by God'.[5]

At first hearing, this second move may seem to lack the religious appeal of the first. If the central concern of the religious man is with God, is it not a fatal abdication for theology to acknowledge its inability to speak of God in himself? Yet this approach also can appeal to a powerful grounding in Christian tradition—especially within Lutheranism. To speak of a knowledge of God in himself, abstracted from our apprehension of him in a relationship of faith and adoration, suggests a detached, spectator attitude, a knowledge of the head rather than of the heart. Even if such a knowledge were possible philosophically, would it not be religiously arid and arrogant? To know Christ is to know his benefits. To limit our knowledge of God to knowledge of his effects as experienced should not, it may be claimed, be seen as an abdication of any vital religious concern, but rather as the safeguarding of a genuinely religious form of knowledge against the pride of human self-assertion.

There are two radical objections often raised against this approach which are based on a misunderstanding of it. It is not a reductionist position in the sense that it identifies God with certain kinds of human experience. God is not, in Schleiermacher's terminology, simply a name for our feeling of absolute dependence; rather 'he signifies . . . for us that which is the co-determinant in this feeling and to which we trace our being in such a state'.[6] God is not, in Tillich's

[5] 'Das Problem einer theologischen Exegese', *Zwischen den Zeiten* 3, 1925, p.353 (cited by W. Schmithals, *An Introduction to the Theology of Rudolph Bultmann*, SCM Press 1968, p.46).

[6] F. D. E. Schleiermacher, *The Christian Faith*, T. & T. Clark 1928, p.17.

language, simply a name for our feeling of ultimate concern; he is that reality of which we are aware when we have an experience of ultimate concern and which we cannot know by any other route. There is a reality other than the human experiencing, but we are only able to speak of it indirectly by speaking of those experiences within which we are aware of its effective presence.

The second misunderstanding is that which sees such an approach as relating God only to man's inner consciousness and not to the world. But this is to misconceive its fundamental intention. On that understanding it would be a matter of seeking to relate God to man's subjectivity; but the rallying cry of existentialist theology has not been to replace objectivity with subjectivity, but to overcome the distinction between the two. It is not that God is related only to consciousness; it is that God is always related through consciousness, through the totality of man's lived experience. Refusal, therefore, to speak of God's relation to the natural order in the way that theology has traditionally done is not a reversion to Gnosticism. It is still the creator God of Christian theism with whom we have to do here, though we are being asked to have to do with him in an unaccustomed mode.

This second move seems therefore more promising. Nevertheless, the difficulties inherent in such an appeal to experience are obvious enough. Experience is not a pure, undiluted substance. One does not have experiences of God whose implications are self-evident and independent of the particular cultural and religious tradition in which one already stands. All our experience is an organic compound of the external world which impinges on us and the kind of person that each one of us is by virtue of our psychological make up and our social and cultural inheritance. In profound or complex experiences at the purely human level—our response to another person, our appreciation of a play, our reaction to some great public occasion—it is not easy to distinguish the contributions of our own mood or character, of the prior expectations with which we approached the event, and of the event itself. We are not entirely unable to make such distinctions. We can compare and contrast our response with that of others; but if those others come from a milieu similar to our own we may still be misled. To someone coming from a wholly different culture the underlying experience itself would have been drastically different. Much more is that true in relation to experience of God. It does not require much study of church history to see how often men have ascribed to God that which subsequent generations have been led to ascribe rather to the time-conditioned outlook of that particular age. Much of what seemed to Anselm, for example, to be necessarily inherent in the apprehension of God as just seems to us to derive from the common assumptions of the feudalism of Anselm's day. Such a recognition does not involve the denial that there was any genuine experience of God in such cases. It does, however, highlight the difficulty involved in making affirmations directly about God on the basis of such experiences. The reticence of those who are unwilling to go beyond speaking of man's existence as determined by God is seen to have much to commend it.

But two things need to be said about this reticence. In the first place, it is no panacea; it is no complete or automatic solution to the problem. If it represents a prudent avoidance of the pitfalls that beset all attempts to distinguish between what is true of God absolutely and what is true of our experience of him, that must not be taken to imply that no comparable difficulties attend the giving of 'an account of man's existence as determined by God'. If one is to move at all beyond the assertion that all human existence is 'existence as determined by God' (and theology would hardly be very interesting if it could not make any such move), then the difficulties remain, even if in a less acute form.

On the other hand, it may be questioned whether that reticence needs to be as absolute as is sometimes claimed. There is an important difference of kind between knowledge of persons and knowledge of things, between an I-thou and an I-it form of cognition. But the difference is not absolute. Personal knowledge of another person, however intimate, involves an element of objectifying knowledge about that person, even if that aspect of the knowing is kept largely dormant and out of sight. Conversely, scientific knowledge, even in the physical sciences, cannot wholly exclude the personal dimension. An approach to the knowledge of God of the kind that we are considering ought not therefore to be regarded as precluding any knowledge about God in himself automatically, as if such knowledge could be ruled out absolutely *a priori* on the ground that it would involve a totally different and alien method of knowing. One may certainly know the effects of something and be able to say very little about the thing itself; it is doubtful whether one can properly claim to know the effects of something and yet be able to say nothing whatever about the thing itself.

Am I then simply returning to the age-old position that rational knowledge of God on the basis of our experience in the world is after all possible, though it must be recognized to be of an indirect and analogical nature? Not entirely. So far, I have simply argued that such knowledge is not to be ruled out in advance as methodologically impossible. Moreover, even if, and in so far as it may be possible, I would want to argue that there is need for a far greater caution, a far more profound awareness of the indirectness of the language than has been customary. In practice there are many who would gladly accept with the fullest conviction and sincerity that all our language about God must be understood as analogical in character, and yet who also believe that it is still possible to develop a clearly structured and coherent set of beliefs about God. The whole structure no doubt bears a uniquely odd relationship to the reality it describes, yet the structure itself can boast firmness and clarity of delineation.

But this is a misplaced confidence. Its nature can be illustrated from contemporary debate between theologians of a classical Thomistic ethos and exponents of a process theology. In his essay 'The Reality of God', Schubert Ogden objects to the classical Western development of theism as one in which we 'find ourselves in the hopeless contradiction of a wholly necessary creation of a wholly contingent world'.[7] Professor Owen defends the conception against the charge of being self-contradictory, while acknowledging that it 'is not one to which we can attach any meaning (that is, positive content) in terms of our experience'.[8] He counterattacks by describing as 'sheer self-contradiction' Ogden's statement in that same original essay that 'one can assert God's independence of the actual world (in his abstract identity) without saying he is wholly external to it, and one can affirm his inclusion of the actual world (in his concrete existence) without denying that the world as actual is completely contingent and radically dependent on him as its sole necessary ground'.[9] Now it seems to me that both sides

[7] Schubert M. Ogden, 'The Reality of God', in *The Reality of God*, SCM Press 1967, p.17.

[8] H. P. Owen, *The Christian Knowledge of God*, Athlone Press 1969, p.246.

[9] H. P. Owen, op. cit., p.105: Schubert M. Ogden, op. cit., p.62.

of this dispute are justified in the criticisms that they raise against the other, but over-confident about the rational viability of their own affirmations. The sources of our knowledge about God may not necessarily rule out all forms of talk about him. They certainly do not seem to me to be of a kind that can appropriately lead to so closely articulated a structure of beliefs as either school proposes.

But if we are to eschew even these forms of sober, scholarly construction of a coherent doctrine of God, does that involve the abdication of reason from all say in our discourse about God? Does it mean an abandonment of theology to the unbridled, and often unsavoury, imaginings of the human mind? The dangers here are great. Nonsense is still nonsense, even when people talk it about God. Contradictions remain contradictions and cannot be rescued from their logical impropriety by the magical device of rechristening them paradoxes.[10] This simple fact is obvious enough, and theologians ignore it at their peril. But it is important also to insist that the criteria for distinguishing between sense and nonsense are not entirely straightforward. The logic that is unequivocally and impartially applicable to all forms of human discourse is minimal indeed. The criteria for determining what is sense and what is nonsense in poetic utterance or in avowals of human love are not on all fours with those that operate in the case of a scientific argument. Where we meet with affirmations that strike us at first hearing as strange or even incoherent, it is our duty before we dismiss them as nonsense to try to see whether they may not be the only available pointers to some new and profound form of

[10] Cf. Ronald Hepburn, 'The Gospel and the Claims of Logic', in *Religion and Humanism*, BBC Publications 1964, p.15; Charles Hartshorne, *The Divine Relativity*, Yale University Press 1948, p.1.

experience. Human experience seems to involve certain antinomies which can only be indicated by a challenging, even violent, wrenching of ordinary linguistic usage. The distinction between such uses of language and mere non-sense is not always easy to define. But it is a distinction that we need to draw and that we do draw. It is in this kind of way that a rational, but not rationalistic, critique of religious and theological language needs to be developed. The increasing range of our knowledge of other religious traditions may be opening up to us the possibility of real progress in this respect. The more we are able to communicate with those whose awareness of God arises out of a religious tradition very different from our own, the better we will be placed to distinguish between the fundamental and the ephemeral, between profound apprehension and gross misconception.

But that is to point forward to a very long-term programme. For the kind of mutual understanding between people of different traditions for which it calls is no superficial one; it is something that can only be built up gradually over a considerable period of time. It is not something to which I myself am in a position to contribute at all. I want, rather, in the second half of this chapter, to ask from within the Christian tradition in a more specific and positive way— what kind of affirmation about God does Christian experience justify? In describing myself as speaking from within the Christian tradition, I do not mean to imply that I am automatically restricted in what I can say about God by any binding rules laid down within that tradition; rather, I am simply recognizing the fact that it is that tradition which inevitably moulds any experience of God which I, and the vast majority of those with whom I have any close contact, have had, and that it is experience of that particular kind from which my theological reflection is inevitably derived.

First, then, everything that suggests the validity of belief in God at all points to belief in his transcendence. The 'absoluteness' of Schleiermacher's feeling of absolute dependence and the 'ultimacy' of Tillich's 'ultimate concern' must be taken with full seriousness. However much it might seem to ease the intransigent problem of evil, there is no possibility of going back on the Christian conviction of creation *ex nihilo*. Implicit in awareness of God is awareness of that which is the source and the ground of everything else. This basic fact is the source of much of our difficulty in using the criterion of coherence in relation to our talk about God. However great our desire to talk coherently about God and about his relation to the world, there is always bound to be an unassimilable 'surd' element in our speech about him. For by definition we are speaking of that which does not and cannot fit within the system for which and from which all our speaking is developed. The point is fundamental, and can be illustrated from the problem of talking about ourselves as persons. We can talk with a reasonable (though limited) measure of precision about how we function as personal beings, how we handle the influences that play upon us and how we react to other people. But there are limiting situations—such as my own conception and birth, the origination of my existing as a person at all, where the normal categories of our speech about persons break down, because those categories are designed to operate within the limits of our existence as persons and are ill equipped to deal with any form of exploration beyond those limits.[11] So at the cosmic level, the fundamentally mysterious nature of all talk about God

[11] Cf. W. H. Poteat, 'Birth, Suicide and the Doctrine of Creation', *Mind* LXVIII, 1959, pp.309–21 (reprinted in D. Z. Phillips, ed., *Religion and Understanding*, Blackwell 1967, pp.127–39).

as creator is bound, logically bound, to remain. We may properly affirm him as creator as a way of indicating that co-determinant reality to which we trace our awareness of the ultimate dependence of ourselves and of all that is. But we need to beware of claiming more for our affirmation than that. Time itself is an inherent part of our dependent existence, and so it seems right to speak, with Augustine, of temporal sequence itself as a part of God's creation rather than of creation as an event in time. Distinctions between God's creative and God's sustaining activity would appear, therefore, to have little secure basis and to be of no great significance. What is indicated by speaking of God as creator is something that is uniformly true of his relation to the world all the time.

This first statement about the nature of belief in God closely corresponds to a basic insight embodied in the traditional cosmological argument for the existence of God. However invalid as a formal inference, its strength lay in its covert appeal to an underlying sense of wonder that there should be anything at all. Closely allied to it is a second element, corresponding to the traditional teleological argument. The world we know not only exists; it is one in which we conceive of and sometimes achieve human goals. We find meaning in things around us by relating them to a variety of finite human purposes. Those purposes may be comparatively isolated and self-contained. Or they may fit together into larger, more complex wholes. Part of the experience of God is experience of that which makes ultimate sense of things, not only in terms of their being there at all but in terms of an overall and ultimate purposiveness in them. This is one of those points at which closer dialogue with other religious traditions may call for some modification. The degree to which the discovery of meaning is linked to the achievement of specific purposes in time would not seem to be identical in all cultures. Nevertheless, I find it hard to conceive that that link will ever be wholly broken. The implications of the sense of purposiveness may come to be seen very differently; I do not think that the sense itself will disappear altogether. It seems reasonable, therefore, to continue to work with it. Now the ultimate character of that purpose which is implicit in the experience of God makes it seem appropriate to envisage it also as something by which God is related to the world and its history as a totality, just as we have seen the concept of creation to be something which relates God in a uniform way to the whole created order. But in the case of the concept of purpose there are additional difficulties. The idea of purpose involves the idea of a changing temporal sequence. The idea of a divine purpose seems, therefore, to require the idea of a varying, non-uniform relation of God to differing occasions in the world. So we need to look more carefully at the way in which this aspect of the experience of God is apprehended.

All experience of God is particular experience because we are particular and finite beings. The concept of God as creator may in the first instance have been taught us by others, but it probably comes alive to us as a result of particular experiences. Those experiences may have their special significance for us because of the outstanding beauty or majesty of the thing experienced; on the other hand, the outward element of the experience may be entirely commonplace, but it may happen to coincide with some moment of psychological or spiritual suggestiveness in us. Yet whatever the origin of such experiences, it is comparatively easy to move from the particular to a universal notion of the world's dependence on God. The universal is in no conflict with the particular; it may even have been fully contained within it. In a similar way, the concept of divine purpose has usually arisen (or come alive where it had previously only been accepted formally) in relation to some particular purpose of outstanding significance, whether at a personal or national level. Can we and should we make the same transition from the apprehension of divine purpose in the particular occasion to the concept of divine purpose as something to be understood in a general and universal manner? Or does the apprehension of divine purpose in the particular occasion require us by its inherent nature to envisage a special and different relationship of God to that particular event or series of events?

First, it should be said that a special relationship of this kind is not to be excluded in advance as logically impossible. The achievements of modern science have tempted many to claim that the observed regularities in the world are of such a kind that the conception of any special relationship of God to particular events is logically excluded. But the claim that a full and complete account of those regularities has been or ever could be given is one that cannot be sustained. The idea of a special relationship of God to particular events within the world, which does not apply equally to all other events, is not therefore something to be ruled out simply on the ground that it would offend against an understanding of the world which is already known to be comprehensive apart from it.

Moreover, the Christian tradition does speak of some occurrences within the world as specially embodying the divine purpose. It is an integral part of that tradition to describe certain specific events as in a special sense 'acts of God'. How ought we to understand such claims?

First, we should recognize that similar language is used in relation to the unquestionably general notion of creation.

God, it is said, clothes the lilies of the field. We do not understand this to mean any particular action of God with regard to each distinct lily or to any particular lily that impresses us with its beauty. We treat it as a poetic expression, though not one, therefore, without serious significance. But we are content to spell out its meaning in terms of God as the ultimate source of all existents (including lilies), together with the conviction that such beauty is a feature in the creative purpose of God for the world as a whole.

The more typical and important uses of this kind of language, however, relate to the particular experiences of individuals or nations. 'It was not you who sent me here, but God,' says Joseph to his brethren (Gen. 45.8). It is God who has raised up Cyrus, says the prophet (Isa. 45.1). How is God's sending of Joseph, his raising up of Cyrus to be understood? Sometimes the story suggests some special causative activity on the part of God—it may be of an overtly miraculous kind. But not always; not indeed normally. It is not, however, the understanding of the ancient writers with which we are primarily concerned. Similar affirmations continue to figure prominently in Christian discourse today—both in relation to the ancient stories and in relation to the contemporary scene. If we speak in such terms, how ought we to understand them? I have argued that the idea of some special relationship of God to particular events is not to be excluded in advance as logically absurd. But logical possibility is not by itself sufficient to justify positive affirmation. Nor do I think that such a positive affirmation can in fact be justified. The experience of divine guidance or divine providence is so frequent and so fundamental to Christian experience that if it were to be understood as always implying special divine causation (however possible theoretically that may be), the occurrences of such special divine activity would have to be so numerous as to make nonsense of our normal understanding of the relative independence of causation within the world. On the other hand, there does not seem to be any insuperable difficulty in choosing rather to interpret such language on the analogy of God's clothing of the lilies. Certain events happen in the world; the possibility of their happening derives (as with all other events) from the absolute dependence of the world as a whole upon God. But particular events by virtue of their intrinsic character or the results to which they give rise give (like the beauty of the lilies) particular expression to some aspect of God's creative purpose for the world as a whole. They are occasions which arouse in us, either at the time or in retrospect, a sense of divine purpose. But that sense does not necessarily entail any special divine activity in those particular events. In so far as it is a genuinely religious sense of purpose to which they give rise, it is by pointing to a purposiveness within the world as a whole.

Talk of God's activity is, then, to be understood as a way of speaking about those events within the natural order or within human history in which God's purpose finds clear expression or special opportunity. Such a view is not deistic in the most strongly pejorative sense, in that it allows for a continuing relationship of God to the world as source of existence and giver of purpose to the whole. It is deistic in so far as it refrains from claiming any effective causation on the part of God in relation to particular occurrences. Yet it seems to me that this view does do justice to the underlying religious experience in at least the very great majority of cases where the Christian tradition speaks of the activity of God. But does it apply to all cases? There is at least one series of events—those that make up the life of Christ—

about which the Christian tradition has always insisted most strongly upon that something more of a special divine action which I have been calling into question. Are there grounds for giving a different account in that particular case? That question raises the fundamental problem of christology, which I propose to discuss in the next chapter. If this means that I am leaving my discussion of the doctrine of God at an extremely incomplete and provisional stage, that is as it should be. For no Christian account of the doctrine of God should be other than extremely incomplete and provisional before it has given careful attention to the issues of christology.

3

THE PERSON OF CHRIST

Scholars are often to be heard debating what is the proper starting-point for theology. Natural theology or the Bible? God or Jesus? Any claim that there is one and only one proper starting point for theology is evidence that the proponent of that claim has not yet grasped how theology has to be done. We cannot approach a study of the existence and nature of God in total independence of the Christian tradition; for that tradition is a part of the world we have to study, and the way we see the world is in part determined by the Christian tradition, whether we are personally committed to the Christian faith or not. We cannot come to the study of the figure of Jesus without some already existing conception of the nature and being of God. There is no one logically necessary starting-point from which the structure of Christian doctrine can be developed in linear succession. A variety of approaches is called for, and no one has absolute priority over all the others.

In any discussion of Christian doctrine, therefore, we are free to choose whether we will begin with the more general questions of belief in God or with the more particular issues concerning the person of Jesus. The only rule that should have absolutely binding force is that these two areas of discussion must be allowed to interact upon one another all the time. This rule I have tried to observe by leaving my discussion about God in the previous chapter in an open and unfinished state. I now want to take up the issues of christology, approaching them in an essentially similar vein. This means that the question with which I shall be concerned is: What kind of belief is appropriate in the light of the evidence available to us about the person and work of Jesus and about the religious claims associated with him as Christ and as Son of God in the Christian tradition?

I want to emphasize at the outset the difference between this way of posing the question and the way in which it is more commonly posed in the writings of contemporary theologians. It more often appears in some such form as: How are we to understand and to express christology today? The assumptions implicit in that kind of formulation can be indicated by quotations from two Roman Catholic writers, to both of whom I referred in the first chapter as outstanding examples of a very radical and open approach to the question of development. In *Sacramentum Mundi*, Karl Rahner defines 'the most urgent task of contemporary Christology' as 'to formulate the Church's dogma—"God became man and that God-made-man is the individual Jesus Christ"—in such a way that the true meaning of these statements can be understood, and all trace of a mythology impossible to accept nowadays is excluded'.[1] Jossua insists that 'at the beginning, and as the basis of all Christianity, stands the *identification* of Jesus Christ . . . God *as* man, God *in* a situation of human freedom the maker of history'.[2] Both writers go on to develop extremely searching

[1] Karl Rahner, 'Jesus Christ', *Sacramentum Mundi*, vol. 3, Search Press 1969, p.196.

[2] J. P. Jossua, 'Rule of Faith and Orthodoxy', *Concilium* 1, 6, 1970, pp.56f.

and valuable discussions of christological doctrine. But are they justified in the point at which they claim one has to start? Any formulation of that kind assumes that the essential content is something given, something already known, and that the heart of our problem is how, in the light of contemporary epistemology, we are to understand and to express that which is already in substance known to us. But, as I argued in the last chapter, it is impossible thus to separate the content of belief from the way in which we come to belief. If we acknowledge that there are differences in the grounds of belief appropriate today, we must be prepared to acknowledge that this may involve differences in the substance of the belief also. On the other hand, this does not mean that we start our enquiry from scratch, without any prior conceptions whatever. Inevitably, and quite properly, we start from within a Christian tradition, which helps to shape both the questions raised and the answers given, though it does not prescribe either at any point. It is itself open to question and to reshaping, and no limits to that questioning or to that reshaping can be laid down in advance.

In saying this I have no desire to prejudge the issue. I am calling into question the church's traditional belief in Christ as both God and man only in the sense that I am insisting that it cannot properly be taken as the starting-point of our enquiry; we have no right to treat it as an unquestionable axiom. I am not calling it into question in the sense of denying that it could conceivably be the conclusion of our enquiry; I do not intend to imply that it is an impossible or an absurd belief. I do think that it is a very difficult belief to understand, even in the very limited sense of being sure that one is not talking nonsense in affirming it. No one, of course, has ever denied that it was a very difficult belief. But the concept of 'incarnation', the term in which we most commonly sum up the belief, is, I think, particularly difficult for us today. The logical subject of incarnation is God or the second person of the Trinity. Written into the concept, that is to say, is the need to start from above; to begin with the being of God and then to consider his becoming man. In other words, it suggests an approach about as far removed as it could be from that which I was developing in the last chapter in relation to the understanding of God, with its emphasis on human life as determined by God and its reluctance to go far beyond that in speaking of God in himself. Consequently, the whole thrust of the word 'incarnation' seems to run counter to the lines of approach towards theological knowledge, which on general grounds we are most inclined to adopt.

But none of this constitutes impossibility. In one way or another incarnational belief has always run counter to the most natural lines of approach to theological knowledge. The church has always recognized the highly mysterious nature of incarnational belief. It has affirmed it none the less, because it felt itself compelled to do so. The evidence, it was convinced, required that and nothing less, however difficult and however strange. That was a perfectly proper procedure. But we too have to be convinced that the evidence requires it. To acknowledge its possibility is not by itself enough—even when supported by centrality within the tradition. The evidence must require it—not in the impossible sense of logical entailment, but in the appropriate sense that the totality of the evidence would be stranger and more inexplicable if the belief were not true than even the acknowledged strangeness of the belief itself. It is that sense of requirement that I want to review.

I propose to begin the enquiry with a general point about

belief in the incarnation. Whatever else may be involved in christological belief (and we shall take up the question of its breadth of reference later), it includes a reference to the specific historical figure of Jesus. It is Jesus who is the Christ; it is the son of Mary who is also the incarnate son of God. It includes, therefore, reference to a particular person at a particular moment in history as the embodiment of the divine, of that which by definition has absolute worth and absolute authority for us. This has never been an easy or readily acceptable claim to make. It had peculiar difficulties for the Greek mind, and those difficulties were a basic cause and feature of much early doctrinal debate. But it also involves a similar, but quite differently grounded difficulty for us today. The rise of modern historical consciousness has, in some degree or another, made historical relativists of us all. By that I mean that when we think and speak most carefully, we recognize the need to assess all statements, especially statements of fundamental belief, in relation to the particular cultural situation of the time. This makes it extremely difficult for us (I am tempted to say impossible, but that would be to prejudge the issue) to ascribe absolute authority to any particular occasion or to any particular set of experiences within the world. This does not, of course, rule out the possibility of giving a very high degree of authority to particular occasions or to particular areas of experience. It would be absurd to suggest that all moments or all experiences were equally significant. If they were, it is questionable whether the term 'significance' could be given any meaning. But even allowing for this vital qualification, the ban on ascribing absolute authority to particular pieces of experience is one that Christians have not found it easy to accept. For the doctrine of the incarnation—if it is to have any practical application to men's lives—might seem to require that we do ascribe such absolute authority to the life of Jesus. If we combine a belief in the doctrine of the incarnation with the conviction that doctrines have work to do—that is to say, that there must be practical implications which follow from them—then we will be inclined to try to find a way round this theoretical difficulty.

It is a very proper and healthy thing to be sceptical of philosophers or others who try to tell us that it is impossible to do something which people appear to have done for a long time and to be continuing to do. The philosopher may still be right because what he is saying is not that it is impossible for people to act in this particular way, but that it is impossible for them to act in this way without being inconsistent with what they do at other times. But people are at times inconsistent—either consciously or, more often, because they are unaware of the full implications of what they do on certain occasions. But at this general level inconsistency is a difficult thing to prove—especially to the satisfaction of the person who seems to us to be being inconsistent and who may have strong reasons for being reluctant to acknowledge the fact. At the theoretical level, therefore, the argument will be difficult to conduct, and unlikely to appear convincing to those who are not already convinced in advance.

But it is not perhaps necessary to pursue the discussion any further at the theoretical level. If we are to give absolute authority to the life of Jesus, we need to have reliable knowledge of that life. This issue has been a central concern for theology, at least since the time of Lessing. This is not the place to survey the vicissitudes of those debates over the last two hundred years. It is, however, the place to attempt some reflection on the implications of those debates. Assessments of the position are notoriously controversial. Disagreement often arises from differing expectations of 'reliability'. In their attempts to distinguish the individual contribution of Jesus from the continuing contribution of the church, New Testament scholars have sharpened their tools to an extreme degree of precision. What has been the outcome of the application of those tools? By the standards to be expected in such historical detective work, they can properly be said to indicate a reasonable degree of reliability in the gospel records. But by those standards one would not expect to be able to distinguish with precision between the role of the founder figure of a movement and the ways in which his person and his teaching have been developed in the continuing tradition. Yet under strong theological pressure (often from within themselves as much as from outside) scholars have been inclined to claim much more than this. In general they have been right to undertake the task; in general the task has been carried out with great sensitivity and insight. What has often been at fault is the claim for a far greater degree of certainty than is justified; than, it would seem, is in practice possible. The great variety of reconstructions offered is evidence against the measure of confidence with which most of them are put forward. Certainly there are lunatic fringe interpretations which can be excluded; there are interpretations to which differing measures of probability can properly be ascribed. But there is still a wide range of possibilities which remain seriously and genuinely open possibilities. And these affect not just details of the teaching of Jesus, but fundamental issues concerning the nature of his mission and his own understanding of it. The 'new quest' of the historical Jesus may have overcome some of the particular problems of the 'old quest'; it has not escaped its fundamental difficulty. Nor is any subsequent quest likely to do so.

It is not, as I have said, my intention to discuss this problem in detail. That is one continuing and vitally important feature of theological scholarship. But it is essential that the doctrinal theologian recognizes the real position with which he has to deal. He has to recognize that the kind of information about Jesus that theology has so often looked to New Testament scholars to provide is not available. And this is not because those scholars are being over-sensitive or unnecessarily sceptical. The information the theologian has traditionally looked for is simply not the kind of information that can properly be expected to be drawn from the evidence at our disposal by historical means. This is something the theologian has simply to accept. There is nothing noble, magnanimous or radical about his doing so. Like Carlyle's interlocutor who said she had decided to accept the universe, he has in fact no option if he wishes his theology to be concerned with the real world and not with some fantasy world of his own creation.

It will now, I think, be clear why I did not consider it necessary to develop in detail my more theoretical affirmation that it is not possible with consistency to ascribe an absolute authority to a particular section of experience within the world, such as the life of Jesus. It was unnecessary because no such isolable section is in fact accessible to us. We do not need to discuss whether it would be philosophically and religiously appropriate to ascribe such authority to Jesus, for no such Jesus is available to us or likely to become available to us. A central part of the task of Christian doctrine today is to work out the implications of this fact for the structure of doctrine as a whole and for christology in particular.

To many a man not only in the pew but in the pulpit, the picture that I have been drawing will, I fear, seem a disturbing one. But theologians are made of sterner stuff. Long acquaintance with the vagaries of the quests for the historical Jesus is likely to produce surprise not at the picture drawn but rather at the fact that I should seem to make so much fuss about it. Did he really expect, they will be inclined to complain, to find substantial evidence for christological affirmation in the history of Jesus? Is he not well aware of the much broader bases that are available to the would-be christologian? Yes, indeed I am aware of them and intend to go on to discuss them. But before doing so I want to issue a warning against healing the wound of my people too lightly. I want to insist that there is an oddity, which we must not allow our sophistication to obscure from us, in affirming of a particular historical person that he is the embodiment of the divine and at the same time acknowledging that our knowledge about him in himself is at every point tentative and uncertain. It means that certain kinds of corollary which might have been expected to follow from that doctrine (and have in fact been understood to follow from it) cannot in fact result from it—even if the doctrine be true. This does not mean that the doctrine would have no practical implications, but that those implications cannot include any absolute guidance in revelation about God or in teaching about human life. Any absoluteness implicit in the concept of an incarnate divine being is necessarily dissipated by the tentativeness of our knowledge of his life and words.

There is a parallel here with the doctrine of God as I set it out in the previous chapter. We know Jesus, as we experience God, only in his effect upon the world, upon the church and upon ourselves. In the case of the doctrine of God I argued that this fact required us to be far less confident in talking about God in himself, in contrast to talking about our life as determined by him, than has been characteristic of the main Christian tradition. The parallel facts about the indirectness and uncertainty of our knowledge about Jesus should make us similarly less confident in our talk about the special relationship of the man Jesus to God, which has been the primary form taken by traditional christological affirmations. We may need to be more ready to rest content with talk about that which we receive through him and to be more reticent in our speech about his own inherent nature. But before we draw such conclusions, we must consider the other areas of evidence to which appeal can properly be made in christology.

If, then, we acknowledge our inability to draw firm lines of demarcation between what is true of Jesus himself and what is true of the initial response to him revealed in the New Testament writings, how should we proceed? There are two main moves open to us. In the first place, we may claim that the historical evidence that concerns us is not simply that of Jesus himself, but the whole event of his life and its impact on the world of the first century. Secondly, we can choose to put increased weight on other kinds of experience—the church's experience and understanding of Christ down the ages rather than historical reconstruction of his life and times. These two moves are in no way incompatible with one another. Indeed, they may even be said to merge into one another, in that a good deal of the witness to Christ in the New Testament lacks that historical immediacy which would most readily differentiate it from the later experience and reflections of the church. Nevertheless, the two moves are sufficiently distinct for us to consider them separately in turn.

A move from concentration upon the individual figure of Jesus to the whole Christ event (to use the convenient, if rather ugly, modern jargon) could be represented as a return to the true centre of Christian concern. Did not St Paul himself say (in perhaps the most over-worked text of this century) that even though he had known Christ after the flesh, yet henceforth he knew him so no more (II Cor. 5.16)? Do not the New Testament scriptures include apostle as well as gospel (to use Marcion's old division)—and indeed numerically more apostle than gospel? Has not the era of objective revelation been traditionally defined as continuing down to the death of the last apostle? All that is true. But in the past it was generally believed that within that totality there existed separable and wholly reliable accounts of the person and the mission of Jesus. If the Fourth Gospel is understood to be a precise record of the *ipsissima verba* of Jesus, its significance as evidence for christology is vastly different from what it is if the gospel is understood in any of the ways in which most modern scholars would regard it. If the epistles of St Paul embody divinely disclosed truths about the divine purpose of Christ's coming, death and resurrection rather than one man's profound wrestling with the impact of Jesus on himself and on his world, then the kind of evidence for christological reflection that they provide is of a very different order. These contrasts are crudely drawn and we are not, of course, confined to a choice between one extreme and the other. But they are, I hope, sufficient to indicate that, though some features of this approach may have close parallels in the past, it is a move to something new; it is not simply a return to the true and familiar path after one hundred and fifty years of aberrant wandering down the false trail of quests for the historical Jesus.

What, then, is the real nature of the evidence with which we have to deal? Our first impression may be one of liberation from the vexing problems involved in a historical study of the gospels. We need not on this approach concern ourselves too anxiously with distinguishing the contribution of Jesus himself and that of the evangelists. If our interest is to be centred on the response of those who acclaimed him in the first century, we have their writings—or the writings at least of some of them—at first hand. Textual problems are there, but despite the ingenious theories of those who see the hand of glossators and later redactors on every page, they do not seem to me unduly serious. Nevertheless, the problems of evaluation and assessment are vast. In this field, once again I can do no more than give a general impression of its overall character with a view to considering what kind of judgment can properly be made in the light of it by the modern christologian.

That the transforming impact of Jesus, of his death and resurrection in particular, is enormous goes without saying. In trying to give some general assessment of its character. it is both natural and helpful to do so in conscious relation to the way in which that evidence has been read in the past, for that reading inevitably affects us all at deep and unconscious levels. Within the Christian tradition, the New Testament has for long been read through the prism of the later conciliar creeds. This has tended to make us see the picture in sharper focus than the picture itself would seem to warrant. This shows itself especially in two ways. In the first place, the forms of response to Jesus and the ways of understanding to which that response gives rise are more varied than has often been recognized. This point should not be over-emphasized. The 'unity' of the New Testament is not a purely imaginary concept. The centrality of the impact of Jesus is well-nigh universal. But the variety of forms that it takes suggests essentially exploratory and provisional patterns of response and understanding. Secondly, the affirmations about Jesus are often much less precise and less absolute than they sound to ears accustomed to the language of later Christian theology. Speaking of Jesus as the Son of God had a very different connotation in the first century from that which it has had ever since Nicaea. Talk of his pre-existence ought probably in most, perhaps in all, cases to be understood, on the analogy of the pre-existence of the Torah, to indicate the eternal divine purpose being achieved through him, rather than pre-existence of a fully personal kind.[3]

As we try to penetrate more deeply into the material, it is possible to see something of the factors that helped to form these varied and developing accounts of Jesus. In doing so we are involved once more in very tentative essays at historical reconstruction. The early Christians were influenced by the transforming character of their experiences and by the categories in which it was natural for them to interpret Jesus and his work. As we have already seen in relation to experience of God, there is no such thing as pure experience; they were only able to experience liberation through Jesus because they already believed him to be in some form or another a vehicle of God from whom liberation was to be hoped for. Nor, on the other hand, were they rationalist theologians, drawing firm deductions from fixed and detailed patterns of expectation; the categories in which it was natural for them to think of Jesus were extended and outgrown by the immensity of the experiences in which they were caught up and which they associated with him as risen Lord.

[3] Cf. G. B. Caird, 'The Development of the Doctrine of Christ in the New Testament', in Norman Pittenger (ed.), *Christ for Us Today*, SCM Press 1968, pp.66–80; John A. T. Robinson, *The Human Face of God*, SCM Press 1973, pp.143–79.

What, then, was it that drove them to speak of him in terms of such absolutist tendency and to associate God's redemptive work so totally with the events of his life, death and resurrection? Here very different judgments are possible. To some it will seem that their accounts run so sharply counter to their monotheistic pre-suppositions that they are only explicable if Jesus was indeed more than a prophet, nothing less than the incarnate Son of God that later orthodoxy has declared him to be. To others it may seem that the apocalyptic expectations of some final cataclysmic act of God for his people, characteristic of the time of Jesus, provide a possible background in the light of which the affirmations about Jesus to be found in the New Testament, however striking, are not wholly inexplicable phenomena.[4] The issue is one of the greatest complexity and difficulty. I can only here declare my own tentative judgment. The move from concentration on the figure of Jesus alone to concern with the whole Christ-event strengthens the case for giving some special evaluation to that series of events as a whole; it does not seem to me to show that this can only be done adequately by giving a special evaluation to Jesus himself of the unique kind that Christian orthodoxy has in fact given. It certainly does not show that evaluation to be false. The fundamental question that it raises is whether our evidence is sufficient to make possible, let alone to require, such a judgment.

But we have already said that our first move need not stand alone, and the church has not usually in practice (whatever it may have claimed to be doing in theory) based its christology exclusively on the witness of the New Testament. Christian interpretation of the New Testament has been powerfully influenced by the experience of redeeming

4 See my 'Looking into the Sun', *Church Quarterly* 3, 1969, pp.196–200.

grace in the lives of later Christians, their practice of worship and the whole developing logic of their understanding of God's relation to the world. In the crucial debates of the Arian controversy it was factors of this kind that convinced the church as a whole that the Athanasian reading of the New Testament evidence was right and that the (not greatly inferior) Arian reading was wrong.[5] It was factors of this kind that ensured that the Reformers, for all their recasting of the tradition and insistence on the New Testament as their sole authority, remained fully traditionalist in christological doctrine. Leonard Hodgson points out that in the debates of the seventeenth and eighteenth centuries 'the unitarians as well as their opponents accepted the Bible as containing revelation given in the form of propositions', and concludes that '*on the basis of argument which both sides held in common*, the unitarians had the better case'.[6] And yet for all that it was not the unitarians who won the day. Christological doctrine has never in practice been derived simply by way of logical inference from the statements of Scripture.

At times the appeal to a broader basis for incarnational belief has been pushed to such extreme lengths as to exclude the need for any form of historical appeal at all. The ways in which this has been done are enormously varied in character. Anselm, more generally famed for his attempt in the ontological argument to demonstrate belief in God without the need for appeal to any empirical premise, undertook the even bolder task of justifying belief in the incarnation, while 'leaving out Christ as if he had never been heard of'.[7] In the *Cur Deus Homo* he set out to show that only

[5] See my *The Making of Christian Doctrine*, Cambridge University Press 1967, p.96.
[6] Leonard Hodgson, *The Doctrine of the Trinity*, Nisbet 1943, pp.220, 223 (italics original).   [7] Anselm, *Cur Deus Homo*, Praefatio.

through a God-man could the honour and justice of God be met—and that since they most certainly must be met, there must be a God-man. Nothing could be further removed from the empirical approach of so much recent theology than this type of Anselmian argument. Yet some modern theologians, in trying to come to terms with the growth of historical uncertainty about the actual figure of Jesus, which I was speaking about earlier in this chapter, have found themselves embarked on a somewhat similar venture. They too have had to turn to sources other than the records about Jesus as the basis for their christological convictions. Tillich is an outstanding example of someone who has followed this line. He claims that 'participation, not historical argument, guarantees the reality of the event upon which Christianity is based. It guarantees a personal life in which the New Being has conquered the old being.' The extreme nature of his position is clearly revealed by the fact that he goes on to argue that it is a consequence of historical method that it cannot be guaranteed that the name of that person was Jesus. But this doubt (which he admits is theoretical rather than real) does nothing to qualify his firm insistence that 'whatever his name, the New Being was and is actual in this man'.[8] He appears, that is to say, to be more confident that there has been an incarnation in history than he is that the name of the incarnate one was Jesus. That fact is a witness to the radical shift that has taken place in the sources of evidence to which appeal is being made.

What, then, are we to say about appeals to evidence of this kind? Their essential character is their use of contemporary understanding or contemporary experience rather than of authoritative witness from the past. Experience and under-

[8] Paul Tillich, *Systematic Theology* 2, Nisbet 1957, p.131.

standing are, as I have insisted many times, closely inter-
related. Our experience is moulded by our understanding,
and our understanding is modified by our experience. In the
course of Christian history, the range of religious experience
that has come to be associated with the name of Christ and
that is therefore apprehended as experience of Christ has
become enormous. The extensive connotation of the term
'Christ' could be illustrated from a vast range of devotional
and theological writing. I take as an example some words
of Emile Mersch, where he puts forward an explanation of
what he means by the phrase 'the whole Christ'. He writes:

> The whole Christ is Christ considered with all that is inseparable from
> Him in the reality of things: with the entire Trinity in which He is one
> God, and with the whole of mankind with which He forms one body,
> His own. This is the *totus et integer Christus* mentioned in the documents
> of our faith; Christ who possesses the fullness of divinity and who is
> the fullness of humanity; . . . this Christ is exactly the same as the
> historical Christ, the same as Jesus, Son of the Blessed Virgin, now
> present in the Eucharist.[9]

Those who write in this vein are not to be accused of
forcing language to meet the particular needs of their
theological scheme. They are truly reflecting the range of
religious experiences associated with the concept of the
Christ. Nor need we call in question the genuinely religious
character of experiences over the whole of that varied range.
But the particular question with which we are concerned
at the moment is how far such experiences can properly be
used to confirm the specific doctrinal scheme within which
they arise and in terms of which they express themselves.
In trying to do this we have always to bear in mind the
warning implicit in some terse words of Don Cupitt: 'It's no
accident that Catholics have visions of Mary, and Buddhists

[9] E. Mersch, *The Theology of the Mystical Body*, Herder 1955, p.51.

have visions of the Buddha.'[10] And conversely, where that degree of specificity is not written in to the experience itself, the descriptions of experience often sound very similar even when coming from within totally different religious traditions; yet these no doubt very real and significant experiences are then seen as confirmation of very different (often mutually exclusive) sets of religious beliefs.

Now in Mersch's case the identification of Christ with the figure of Jesus is a part of the tradition with which he begins. The impact of his writings is to show that that identification contributes to a religious tradition of great spiritual power. But I do not see that the acknowledged power of that tradition alters the initial status of the claimed identification; it cannot be allowed to confirm it as a truth demanding universal acceptance. For it is not the only religious tradition of great spiritual power. And it is precisely this aspect of the Christian tradition, this absolute identification of all that has come to be implied by the term Christ with the figure of Jesus, that is being called into question by inter-religious debate, as well as by reflections within Christianity itself of a kind that I have been raising earlier in this chapter. The point is made explicitly by Raymond Panikkar in his *Unknown Christ of Hinduism*.

Hinduism and Christianity will agree to some extent that both meet in God and that God is working inside both religions as it were. The Christian claim is that God and Christ are indivisible and inseparable, though yet without mixture and fusion, and that where God is at work in this world as it were it is always in and through Christ that he acts. Hinduism would not find too much difficulty in accepting this and would call it perhaps Isvara (Lord). The stumbling-block appears

[10] C. F. D. Moule and Don Cupitt, 'The Resurrection: A Disagreement', *Theology*, October 1972, p.509.

when Christianity further identifies, with the required qualifications, Christ with Jesus the Son of Mary.[11]

How, then, are we to assess the validity of this (suitably qualified) identification? The historical evidence which we surveyed in the earlier part of the chapter remains tantalizingly ambiguous. The quality of experience, *qua* experience, associated with the belief in later Christian tradition is, I have argued, too indirect and too variegated to be of service here. Confirmation, if it is to be found, must be looked for rather in reflection on what must be true to make sense of the religious understanding of the world as a whole to which the Christian tradition points. If the concept of a specific incarnation in the person of Jesus is the pivot on which the whole tradition of a communion between man and God in Christianity has been based, both intellectually and devotionally, we might find ourselves forced to choose between some form of its traditional affirmation on the one hand and the abandonment of any positive and coherent understanding of the Christian tradition on the other. It is in these terms that John Baker, for example, defends a doctrine of 'Incarnation in the full, traditional import of the term'. He sums up his argument forcefully in these words: 'Without the Incarnation Christianity is both incoherent and inadequate; and with the Incarnation Christianity shows up the incoherence and inadequacy of non-incarnational theism.'[12] When the issue is posed in these terms, it is evident that the question of christology cannot be settled in isolation. It interacts so closely with the

[11] Raymond Panikkar, *The Unknown Christ of Hinduism*, Darton, Longman and Todd 1965, pp.23f.

[12] John Austin Baker, 'Behaviour as a Criterion of Membership', in John Kent and Robert Murray (eds.), *Church Membership and Intercommunion*, Darton, Longman and Todd 1973, p. 134.

more general question of our knowledge of God and of his relation to the world that any further progress on the specifically christological issue must proceed *pari passu* with progress on our unfinished discussion of the more general issue of the knowledge of God and of his relation to the world.

4

THE WORK OF CHRIST

The position reached at the end of the previous chapter may be put like this. However difficult it may be to show how the doctrine of the incarnation is required by the various particular experiences of which the New Testament speaks or by the various particular experiences which have been characteristic of later Christians, it may none the less be required in order to make sense of the distinctive nature of Christian experience as a whole. It is that question which I want to discuss now. And I want to do so not in terms of revelation, which has been the aspect primarily in mind in the discussion so far, but rather in terms of redemption or atonement. The Christian tradition has never believed that men needed only to be shown the truth about God and about human life. Sin has usually been regarded as more fundamental than ignorance. Men need not only to be enlightened; they need to be changed. The forgiveness and the transformation of man are at least as basic to Christ's mission as the impartation of knowledge and illumination. Is there, in the understanding of this area, evidence which shows the necessity of an incarnational doctrine?

'Christ,' said Whitehead, 'gave his life; it is for man to

discern the doctrine.'[1] The two millennia of Christian history bear witness to men's failure in discernment. The history books are littered with doctrinal accounts of the atonement which strike us as absurd or immoral or both. And such judgments are not only, or at least not always, the falsely superior judgments of men from a later period of history; they were not infrequently the judgments of contemporaries. Eucharistic doctrine also, another facet of the discerning of the doctrine of Christ's self-giving, has been at least as divisive of Christians from one another as anything else in the last one thousand years. Our own age, in consequence, is probably more disillusioned about the possibility and the value of doctrinal statement in this area than in any other. The story of the passion retains its appeal; any doctrine of the passion is more likely to appal. But one cannot respond to the passion without some pattern of understanding. However disenchanted we may feel with past attempts, we cannot simply refuse the endeavour to understand. And as soon as we give any coherent shape to that understanding, we have embarked on the paths of doctrine, whether we will it or no.

The ancient church did not formulate its doctrine of the atonement with the same kind of precision that it brought to bear on the subject of christology. It was happy to give expression to its faith at this point with the aid of a rich mixture of pictorial images. But there was a firm central core of faith to which those images were giving expression. That central core, though not precisely defined, was most firmly held. It can fairly be conveyed as a belief that in the death and resurrection of Christ God had worked effectively in history to transform once for all man's status (or at the

[1] Alfred North Whitehead, *Religion in the Making*, New York: The Macmillan Co. 1926, p.45.

very least man's potential status) in relation to God. This has been generally accepted ever since as that to which any doctrine of the atonement must do justice, the primary criterion by which its adequacy is to be judged. It is on this ground that so-called 'subjective' theories are seldom allowed more than a wistful acknowledgement of some valuable insights in what is judged to be their partial and truncated accounts of the atonement. Leonard Hodgson described 'the main theme' of his book on *The Doctrine of Atonement* as being 'that the doctrine of the atonement proclaims an objective act of God whereby the power of evil in creation has been overcome and cast out, a mighty act for which the idea of a military victory gives an appropriate and illuminating analogy'.[2] A few pages later he reiterates the same point with renewed emphasis. 'Both in theory and in practice,' he writes, 'we need to maintain at the heart of the doctrine of the atonement the message of an objective atonement wrought once for all by God in the history of this world, in virtue of which things are not as they were.'[3] It is the possibility and the implications of this kind of claim that I want to consider.

I referred in the previous chapter to the apocalyptic context within which the life and ministry of Jesus was lived and understood as being an important contributory factor in giving rise to the absolute nature of the claims made about him. If, then, his death and resurrection were seen in any sense as redeeming acts of God, they would naturally be seen as final and ultimate acts of God. They would overshadow everything from the past, leading indeed to the view that all earlier redemptive acts of God were types or shadows of this final act. And no further future redemptive

[2] Leonard Hodgson, *The Doctrine of the Atonement*, Nisbet 1951, p.146.
[3] Ibid., p.149.

act in any sense parallel to this one would be envisaged, because no future of any extended kind was envisaged at all. The redemptive act in Christ would appear both literally and metaphysically ultimate.

But if that was a contributory source to the understanding of Christ's redemption as a once-for-all unrepeatable act of God, the understanding itself not only survived but grew stronger with the fading of the apocalyptic hope. Were there then any features in the various ways in which redemption came to be understood which strengthened and maintained the conviction of its once-for-all objective character? And if there were, do they continue to have force for us, even when the apocalyptic context has become one with which we can no longer identify ourselves?

Four pictures were of particular importance to the early church in its thought about the atonement, and all of them have continued to figure prominently in later theorizing. These are the understanding of it as a victory over Satan, as meeting the just demands of divine law, as the offering of a sacrifice and as a reversal of the sin of Adam. I want to begin with a brief consideration of the significance of each of these, asking whether their inner meaning requires the concept of 'an objective act of God . . . in the history of this world, in virtue of which things are not as they were'.

The first picture, that of victory over the devil, is precisely the picture which Hodgson himself selects as an appropriate analogy to indicate the decisive and objective character of the atonement. The picture has always required careful qualification in Christian thought, because Christianity is not in the last analysis a dualistic faith. The devil is not an equal adversary; the eventual outcome of the struggle is never in doubt. God is the source and Lord of all; and he will be all in all. Nevertheless, with that qualification the picture could be allowed to stand. And in the demon-ridden world in which the Christian gospel was first preached, it was not merely a possible but an extremely powerful picture. But the implications of this analogy for doctrine will vary in accordance with one's beliefs about the ontological status of Satan and the demons. That is an area of belief in which some form of demythologizing is widely accepted today. The reality and importance of the kinds of experience with which such beliefs were linked in the early church should not be underestimated. It is important to recognize that evil is more than a matter of the wrong choices of individuals. It operates through unconscious psychological forces and large-scale sociological pressures. The moral evil that grips us has a supra-personal dimension, surpassing not only our practical control but our theoretical understanding also. Thus the area of experience indicated by scriptural talk of the devil and of evil forces continues to be one that needs to be taken seriously. But the nature of those experiences does not seem to point to supernatural personal forces in a way comparable to that in which the experience of good points towards the reality of God. Now if the personification of evil forces is abandoned, the image of victory over the devil may still be a valuable picture, assuring us of the ultimate inability of evil even in its most potent and inexplicable manifestations to destroy the personal being of man in God's world. But it is difficult to see how it could require—or even suggest—that that assurance should depend on some act of God in the history of the world in virtue of which things are not as they were.

The concept of law in atonement theory has to face a similar difficulty. It cannot be understood as something that exists on its own over against God, something with which he has to come to terms willy-nilly. It is not a decree which God made in some moment of rash utterance and by which, to his chagrin, he has to stand bound ever after as his pledged word. It can only mean those principles which are necessary for the achievement of the genuinely personal realities which are God's purpose for the world. Of these principles we know something through living as persons in the world. Moral evil disrupts social harmony; it cannot simply be ignored, condoned or treated as of no consequence. To speak of it as sin is to see it as that which disrupts the social framework of God's intended order; still less in such a context is it something to be ignored, condoned or treated as of no consequence. In human society, the control of the social effects of evil requires the operation of law. At times that law has to operate in terms of fixed penalties which must be met before any further, more constructive steps can be undertaken. This is necessary and sometimes beneficial. But we recognize it as a blunt instrument, unavoidable for us because of our lack of insight into human motivation and our need for short term deterrence. But it is an aspect of our experience of law which makes little sense when applied analogically to God's dealings with the world. In that context the concept of the fixed penalty that must be met is crude to the point of absurdity. Once again we are led to say that the ideas associated in Christian thought with an understanding of Christ's death as a meeting of the just demands of the law are not to be dismissed as of no significance. But it is precisely those elements within such ideas which suggest the need for a once-for-all objective act that appear most inappropriate and most lacking in cogency.

The concept of sacrifice, for all its complexity, does not raise any fundamentally different issues. It was a basic religious practice throughout the ancient world and a natural category in which to depict the religious importance of Christ's death. But it was a matter of practice rather than of theory; many different theories (or none) could be associated with it. Those which suggested the necessity for a 'full, perfect and sufficient sacrifice', 'one oblation . . . once offered', did so on principles similar to the legal analogy which we have just been considering. The Epistle to the Hebrews can declare that 'without the shedding of blood, there is no forgiveness' (9.22). But that is no immutable divine principle of life; it is rather the culturally conditioned way in which the Jews at that time gave expression to the seriousness of sin and the costliness of the way to overcome it which they believed God to have provided for them through the law. The category of sacrifice was a natural image to use in relation to the death of Christ. But it does not disclose for us any grounds for claiming the necessity of some act 'once for all, in the history of this world' by which 'God, who is both the source and the object of all the acts of His creatures, has won the right to forgive their sins without the least diminution of His eternal goodness which is the ground of all our hopes.'[4]

The contrasting parallel with the sin of Adam goes back to the widely diffused New Testament concept of Christ as second Adam, and was a prominent co-ordinating theme of much early Christian thought. The two conceptions interacted upon one another. The use of the Adam story as a form of theodicy, explaining man's responsibility for the presence of sin in a world of God's creation, is more marked in early Christian than in contemporary Jewish treatments of the story. To fulfil that role the story needs to be understood in a historical and not merely a symbolical

[4] Leonard Hodgson, op. cit., p.83.

way. This would be a natural way to view the story when it is being seen in parallel with the historical event of Christ's death. But it in its turn could then serve to strengthen and to justify the Christian conviction of a universal significance in that historical event. If the single historical occasion of Adam's sin could entail universal human sin and guilt, then it was appropriate that the single historical event of Christ's death should have a similarly universal redemptive significance. But the parallel can only provide support for the understanding of the atonement as a single historical event with universal effect if the fall is being understood as a single historical event with universal repercussions. Now it is precisely this element of historicity which it is impossible for us today to accept in relation to the Adam story, whatever value we may continue to attach to it as myth. This does not, of course, rule out the possibility of continuing to hold to the traditional insistence on Christ's atoning death as a single historical event with universal significance. What it does mean is that no support for that conviction can be found in the understanding of it as a reversal of the sin of Adam.[5]

The kind of criticisms which I have been making of the traditional pictures of the atonement are not hard to make and are often made. The purpose of this brief review of them is to emphasize one thing. The points at which these pictures are most open to criticism are precisely those points at which they might seem at first to show the necessity of some once-for-all objective act of atonement. If they have contributed to the rise of that conviction in the past, we cannot find in them support for it now. That is not, of

[5] See my 'Does Christology rest on a Mistake?', *Religious Studies* VI, 1970, pp.69–76 (reprinted in S. W. Sykes and J. P. Clayton, eds., *Christ, Faith and History*, Cambridge University Press 1972, pp.3–12).

course, to suggest that they are now incompatible with such a view. But they do not stand or fall with it. They could still stand without it—in, of course, the pictorial sense in which alone they can stand at all. In our search for grounds which inescapably require us to interpret Christ's death in such absolute, objective terms we must look elsewhere.

Within the Christian tradition, Christ's death has not been associated exclusively with sin and its forgiveness. That has been its primary interpretation, but it has always been understood also to have something to say about the problem of human suffering. In the early centuries theologians tended to handle this subject with a defensive caution. Their principal concern was to make clear that the one who secured man's redemption through his passion and death on the cross was none other than the eternal and coequal Son of God. If he were anything less than that, man's redemption would be unavailing. This led to a reluctance to associate his godhead too directly with the human suffering of the passion for fear it might undermine belief in the full, substantial divinity of the redeemer. God and the suffering had in subtle ways to be held apart from one another. The divine Son was indeed the subject of the suffering, but in a way that left untouched the essential impassibility of his divine nature. Such an approach was bound to inhibit any full development of the significance of Christ's cross for the issue of human suffering.

Modern writers have tended to feel less constraint in this matter. The more the problem of suffering has come to be regarded as the most searching challenge to theistic faith, the greater the importance of this aspect of the passion has been felt to be. What beliefs about the passion are needed if it is to fulfil this vital role in Christian theism? Is a fully realistic form of incarnational belief, an insistence on the distinctive presence of the eternal God in the person of Christ, an essential prerequisite if it is to do so?

The issue at stake can be brought into clear focus by a comparison of quotations from two twentieth-century theologians, who despite great differences are at one in their evaluation of the importance of this issue. The first quotation is from Karl Rahner's essay, 'Current Problems in Christology':

How many sorrowful souls have been comforted and have seen through their tears the everlasting stars of love and peace because in their faith they knew 'He, the eternal meaning of the world, the Word, has wept with me, He too has drunk of the chalice.' How many have died 'piously in the Lord' with the thought that this common and general death must mean something just because the Uncommon, the uniquely important, the absolutely Indiscutable, the incommunicable Measure, the coherent Meaning at the heart of being, because He—really He himself—died. 'One of the most Holy Trinity has suffered', the Scythian monks used to say, with that brutality of faith which takes not only death but its hidden divinity with the same seriousness, so that hundreds of years after Ephesus and Chalcedon we are still startled by it, though it is perfectly obvious that we are bound to speak like this and that the whole truth, the single unique truth of Christianity, is contained in it.[6]

My second quotation comes from the final chapter of Hastings Rashdall's history of atonement doctrine:

A God who could contemplate such a world as ours without suffering would not be a loving God, nor would He be in the least like Christ. God must suffer with and in the sufferings of all His creatures . . . And if there has been a supreme manifestation of God in one human being, in one human Personality who once lived on earth and now lives eternally in a supreme union and communion with God, then we may find a special meaning—at least a symbolical meaning—in the

[6] Karl Rahner, 'Current Problems in Christology', *Theological Investigations* I, Darton, Longman and Todd 1966, p.177.

language which treats His sufferings as being, or at least in a pre-eminent sense representing, the sufferings of God himself.[7]

Both are agreed that theism is only tolerable if we are able to speak of a self-identification of God with the sufferings of mankind. Both believe that they are able to do this on the basis of the sufferings and death of Christ. For Rahner this involves being able to speak of the suffering as the suffering of 'one of the most holy Trinity'; it must be 'He, really He himself, who died'. For Rashdall, it is enough to under-stand such language as having 'at least a symbolical mean-ing'. Can we find any form of reasoning which might help to discriminate between these two differing judgments?

Two issues appear to be involved, the first epistemological, the second ontological. The first question is whether Rahner's interpretation is necessary if we are to have reason-able grounds for belief in God's self-identification with the sufferings of man. We have already seen something of the extreme difficulty involved in any assertion of belief about God in himself. Historically it does not seem to be the case that the idea stems exclusively from the fact of Christ. The evidence for any approach to it before the time of Christ is admittedly slender. But adumbrations of it are to be seen in, for example, the prophet Hosea. It seems to me most reasonable to see the early chapters of Hosea as more than mere allegory, as reflecting experiences in the life of the prophet himself. The writing is allusive and the exegetical problems are well known, but it does not seem too fanciful to claim that it was the pain of Hosea's continuing love for his unfaithful wife which gave rise to the distinctive em-phasis in his oracles on the compassionate love of Yahweh for his erring and suffering people. Such a conviction about

[7] Hastings Rashdall, *The Idea of Atonement in Christian Theology*, Macmillan 1919, p.453.

God remains on any assumption an unproven judgment of faith. But it does not seem impossible that it could have arisen from essentially human experiences of suffering, and could be as reasonably grounded on them as any other aspect of our belief about God.

The more important question is whether Rahner's interpretation is necessary not merely for our coming to hold the belief but more basically for the belief in fact to be true. Does Rahner's understanding imply a more complete self-identification on the part of God than is implied by a symbolic interpretation? On the face of it it does. But it is possible that we are being misled here by the abstract nature of the concept 'suffering'. Suffering is not some single entity in which different people share. There is my suffering and your suffering—and they are of many kinds. If the eternal drank of the chalice in the sufferings of the passion, in how direct a sense is that the same chalice as the one drunk by the mother of a brain-damaged child or the chance victim of a psychopathic assault? The suffering in which the eternal Word shares directly can only be a sacramental representation of his self-identification with the sufferings of other individuals. The self-identification itself must be of a different order. It is the truth or otherwise of our speech about that continuing self-identification of God with the sufferings of men and women that is vital to the health of theism. The truth or otherwise of that conviction is not determined by the truth or otherwise of a different order of divine self-identification with suffering in the person of Jesus. There does not seem to be any ground for claiming that the former is either causally dependent on or qualitatively transformed by the latter.

So far we have been considering what must be the case for Christ's passion to be the effective redeeming power in relation to sin and suffering which Christians have claimed it to be and as which Christians continue to experience it. But there is a third fundamental area of human need to which Christ's passion is both affirmed to be and experienced as an answer—it meets man's need in relation not only to sin and suffering, but to sin, suffering and death. In the tradition it is not uncommon to speak in powerful, if paradoxical, terms of Christ's death as the overcoming of human death. But it is clearly the death and resurrection of Christ taken together that are most naturally understood to embody the effective antidote to the fear and fact of death. The same indeed is true, in only slightly less obvious a manner, in relation also to sin and suffering. And it might be objected to the course of the discussion so far that of course it has failed to lay bare the necessity of 'an objective atonement wrought once for all by God in the history of this world', because it has concentrated attention exclusively on one part of that atoning act, and that, in omitting explicit reference to the resurrection, it has in fact neglected precisely that aspect of the atoning act in which its once-for-all transforming power is most clearly and most effectively present. This omission, then, must be rectified. Let us now take up the issue of the resurrection in relation to Christ's redeeming work as embodying the answer to death as a fundamental problem of human life. Does careful attention to this aspect of the matter show in any more conclusive way the inescapably unique character of God's act in Christ?

Now it has certainly been claimed often enough in Christian history that it is through the resurrection of Christ and through that alone that we have grounds for believing in a life after death, and that we have the possibility of participation in it. But such a claim needs careful scrutiny. I have already argued in relation to suffering that historically it did not require the suffering of the incarnate Christ to give birth to the conviction of God's involvement in the tragedy of human suffering, but that that truth was grasped by the prophet Hosea on the basis of his own experience. Similarly, and more clearly, it did not require the resurrection of Christ to give birth to the conviction that God raises the dead. That conviction also can be found in the later strands of the Old Testament tradition, in for example the book of Daniel, as a result of reflection on the human experiences of persecution and of martyrdom. Historically speaking, the resurrection of Jesus was not the initiating ground or the sole source of the resurrection hope.[8]

Nor indeed has it now become so. The fact that we may now be in a position where we feel able to speak of Christ's resurrection as an event in past history does not enable us simply to brush aside those earlier intimations of the resurrection hope as historically interesting but no longer theologically important. For that to be the case we would have to have adequate grounds for affirming the resurrection of Christ today which were entirely independent of them. And that would only be possible if we were to take a wholly uncritical view of Scripture and of the Christian tradition. Once that is ruled out, it is clear that belief in Christ's resurrection cannot simply stand on its own feet. What is meant by the resurrection of Christ is not simply the resuscitation of a corpse; Jesus does not revive to die later like Lazarus or the widow of Nain's son. It is a crossing of the boundary of death absolutely and for all time. It is not, therefore, a historical event on all fours with the passion and the crucifixion. The grounds for our acceptance of it

[8] See pp.130–2 below, where the argument of this and the following paragraph is more fully developed in relation to belief in the resurrection of the body.

will have to be even more complex in character than the grounds for accepting more straightforward historical beliefs. In the process of assessing critically the complex evidence that is appropriate to a reflective affirmation of belief in the resurrection, we are bound to take into account the more general evidence that makes the idea of resurrection in the first instance even a conceivable possibility deserving our consideration, let alone our assent. The reasons that led to the first emergence of such a belief in any form still have their part to play.

Moreover, even at the level of more directly historical evidence relating to the particular event itself, we have to acknowledge that full range of historical difficulties which affect, as we saw in the last chapter, other aspects of the traditions about Jesus also. The Cambridge Divinity Faculty affords striking evidence of how these lead different scholars to very different conclusions. Professor Moule has on a number of occasions set out forcefully his reasons for believing that 'the argument from the existence of the Church to the rightness of the Christian estimate of Christ can be stated in such a way as to make it proof against the obvious attack—namely, that the mere existence of a body proves nothing as to the correctness of its tenets'. For him there 'are well-attested beliefs, to account for which I have to invoke something beyond history, something transcendent. The New Testament calls it the resurrection of Jesus.' Moreover, within that evidence 'the story of the empty tomb is not altogether easy to dismiss as a late, apologetic development'.[9] Professor Lampe, while agreeing that the resurrec-

[9] C. F. D. Moule, *The Phenomenon of the New Testament*, SCM Press 1967, p.19; id., 'The Resurrection: A Disagreement' (with Don Cupitt), *Theology*, October 1972, p.509; id. (ed.), *The Significance of the Message of the Resurrection for Faith in Jesus Christ*, SCM Press 1968, p.9.

tion 'was an event in the external world', 'a fact attested by a series of events which those who experienced them described, in so far as they could be described in human language, by saying that Jesus "appeared to them" or "was seen by them" alive', finds 'the historical arguments' against accepting the story of the empty tomb 'quite compelling'.[10] Don Cupitt's position is different yet again; for him 'ratiocination comes first, and vision second', 'the Easter faith was born by theological and existential reflection upon the completed life of Jesus'.[11] Nor, of course, do these three positions exhaust the possibilities of reasonable historical reconstruction, though they will suffice for our present purposes. Each admittedly has its own historical difficulties. I do not find it easy to judge between them. I incline towards the second or third rather than the first line of explanation; I am certainly not convinced that Christian faith in the resurrection simply could not have arisen in the way assumed by Don Cupitt's interpretation. But my own inclinations in this respect are not directly relevant to the argument, and would require far more detailed historical and philosophical justification than would be appropriate here. What is much more relevant is my conviction (and of this I feel a good deal more confident) that any of the three positions is fully compatible with holding the belief that a God-given resurrection is the answer to human finitude and death, and also fully compatible with that belief being true. If I am justified in that conviction, then we have to say that even the hope of resurrection is not logically dependent on

[10] G. W. H. Lampe and D. M. Mackinnon, *The Resurrection*, Mowbrays 1966, pp.30, 58.

[11] C. F. D. Moule and Don Cupitt, art. cit., pp.516, 509. For a fuller development of his position see Don Cupitt, *Christ and the Hiddenness of God*, Lutterworth Press 1971, ch.10.

invoking 'something beyond history, something transcendent' in the resurrection event of a kind which we would not properly invoke in relation to any other event in history.

At the close of the last chapter I cited John Baker's insistence on the absolute essentiality of a full incarnational doctrine for any coherent and adequate form of theism. When he elaborates that argument in his book, *The Foolishness of God*, he does so in relation to the two themes of suffering and death which I have just been discussing. It is worth asking, therefore, what it is that leads him to draw the opposite conclusion to that which I have drawn.

In relation to suffering, he rightly insists that it would be absurd to suggest that the incarnation was necessary for God to suffer at all. 'The tremendous moment of self-sacrifice, when God voluntarily surrendered perfect joy, was not the moment when an infant was conceived in the womb of a Jewish girl, but when the adventure of creation began. The purpose of becoming Man was not to enable God to suffer, but to bring that suffering into such a relationship with Man that Man could know it, respond to it, and co-operate with it.'[12] It is the logic of the last clause which, despite its obvious attractiveness, does not seem to me compelling—and that for reasons I have given. Up to a point we can know it even without the suffering of the incarnate as Hosea did. To know it fully involves knowing it in relation to my own particular sufferings and the particular sufferings of each individual—and that, I have argued, requires something more than the affirmation of the suffering of the incarnate. The value of the belief in this context is not to be denied. Its necessity, which is the issue under discussion, does not seem to have been established.

[12] John Austin Baker, *The Foolishness of God*, Darton, Longman and Todd 1970, p.309.

In the case of the resurrection, two main points of difference emerge. In the first place, John Baker is much more confident than I feel able to be that the resurrection 'as an objective event' is to be included among those 'aspects of the story of Jesus of Nazareth' which can 'reasonably demand our assent to them as historical realities' after a 'detailed historical critique' of the evidence.[13] This judgment is central to his argument. It is because the resurrection of Jesus is 'so solid a fact' that it can transform the Christian hope (hope not merely of life after death, but of the ultimate triumph of the divine purpose for good) from 'hypothesis' to 'faith' or from 'hope' to 'certainty'. Yet he readily admits that 'conversely, if Jesus had not been vindicated, and in a way which demanded a divine action as its cause, the glorious hope would not have been destroyed, but it would have remained—a hope'.[14] But is it so clear that 'hope' in this sense may not in fact be the very form of faith by which we have to live?

But there is an objection of a more general kind that may be raised against the line of argument that I have been pursuing in this chapter. The whole enterprise, it might be claimed, is misconceived. Evil, suffering and death are irrational; they do not make sense to us. It is precisely this fact about them that constitutes them fundamental problems for our understanding of human life. It is therefore absurd, it may be argued, to search for a logical account of the way in which God deals with them in the world. The objection is not without force, but in seeking to deal with it we need to recall how we have come to take up the discussion.

The Christian tradition cannot be accepted as true, just because it has developed in the particular way that it has—

---

[13] Ibid., p.276.   [14] Ibid., pp.274, 277f., 278f.

however well supported by ecclesiastical authorization or popular piety. The tradition did not come down from heaven, fully developed like Athene from the head of Zeus. It has been developed by men as their understanding of the world of their experience. We cannot, therefore, be exonerated from asking whether they had good reasons for understanding it as they did. That question may well be unanswerable. In that case, there is a further question that we have to ask in relation to a religious tradition of such persistence and of such spiritual power as the one with which we are here concerned. If we have doubts about its traditional doctrinal formulations, are we able to give any alternative account which would be less open to such doubts and which would still do justice to the things that the earlier doctrinal affirmations had enshrined? These are the questions with which I am trying to deal—and it is the second question on which I want now to concentrate attention.

Two features seem to me to find a place in all forms of atonement theory. The first is that Christ's passion is in some way a demonstration of what is true of God's eternal nature. This is clearly true of those who see in it an objective act of God himself. There is no wedge between God's acts and his nature. What he does must be expressive of what he is. Whatever else they may feel needs to be said about the atonement, it will certainly include this affirmation. Those who have criticized such so-called objective theories have usually done so because either they cannot accept or they cannot attach any meaning to that something more. They have not wished to deny that the death of Christ exemplifies the love of God. That indeed has been the heart of what they have themselves wanted to affirm.

The second feature is one less often given explicit mention in any discussion of atonement doctrine, but which is normally assumed and should, I think, be made more explicit. That is the recognition that the passion of Christ has been remarkably effective as a historical phenomenon in the transformation of human lives. Christianity is always in a quandary in any apologetic appeal to historical results. They are not negligible, but they are ambiguous, and certainly do not go far in justifying any absolutist or divine claims that the church may want to make. And this applies to the passion as well as to any other aspect of the faith. It has given rise to morbid and masochistic responses as well as to those which we would judge to be spiritual transformations of a profoundly impressive and valuable kind. But we are not using the notion here apologetically so much as simply descriptively. If it is objected that subjective theories of the atonement are inadequate, because for them the passion is merely exhibitive and not performative, because they do not allow that the passion actually does anything— that objection cannot be sustained in any complete way. In the world of historical experience, the passion has done much and continues to do much; nor are there grounds for limiting its potential effectiveness in the future.

Now that may seem too obvious and platitudinous to be worth insisting on. My reason for doing so is to make the suggestion that it may in fact be to this kind of effectiveness that we should look, if we are conscious of something lacking in traditional subjective theories. May it be that what we need is precisely a combination of these two things: a demonstration of that which is eternally true about God and effectiveness as a historical phenomenon in producing an appropriate response to that truth about God?

At the outset of this chapter I took Leonard Hodgson's book, *The Doctrine of the Atonement*, as an example of a sensitive but uncompromising insistence on the need for an 'objective atonement wrought once for all by God in the history of this world, in virtue of which things are not as they were'.[15] At one point in that book he expresses himself in a form which has a very similar structure to that which I am now proposing. 'In the incarnation,' he writes, 'we think of God as entering into the history of this world not merely to illustrate what He is doing eternally, but to accomplish something which shall contribute to what has gone before and have a permanent effect on what comes after.'[16] But he makes it quite clear that the something accomplished is not simply a matter of straightforward historical causation. Any such theory 'implies that Christ's atoning death is only relevant to the sins of the comparatively small proportion of mankind which has heard of and responded to the preaching of the cross. It lacks the note of "something accomplished, something done", in virtue of which God's forgiveness is ready and waiting for the penitent sinner.'[17]

But what is this elusive something more, which he, and the majority of Christian theologians with him, is so insistent to maintain? Certainly we need to hold firmly to the two aspects: eternal representation and historical effectiveness. Either by itself would be woefully inadequate. Moreover, we need to see them not as two quite distinct and separate things; we need them combined in an effective religious synthesis. In spirituality the two are most effectively combined in sacramental experience. The baptismal and eucharistic sacraments both combine certain underlying features of basic human experience with a specific historical reference to the things concerning Jesus. The two are powerfully fused in a way that led Oliver Quick to claim that 'the

---

[15] Cf. p.63 above.
[16] Leonard Hodgson, *The Doctrine of the Atonement*, p.83.
[17] Ibid., pp.83f.

sacramental outlook enables us to perceive how it is that both the philosopher and the historical critic are apt to miss the real point of the Christian faith'.[18]

May it not be precisely a combination of that kind which traditional objective language about the atonement is designed to express? And if that is its real status and its real purpose, then we are chasing a will o' the wisp if we continue to search for some third distinctive kind of thing which has been accomplished over and above the two contained in my proposed analysis. What that analysis has been designed to show is that it may not after all be as impossible as it is usually assumed to be to do justice to the rightful concerns of atonement doctrine within the apparently more limited framework of christological belief towards which the argument of the previous chapter was pointing us.

[18] Oliver C. Quick, *The Christian Sacraments*, Nisbet 1932, p.57.

5

GRACE AND THE HOLY SPIRIT

The central issue with which we are concerned in this whole study is the question: what ought one to believe about God and his relation to the world in the areas of central importance to Christian faith? I began by considering the fundamental belief in God as the ultimate source of existence and of meaning in the world. This led into a brief discussion of the possibility of divine action in the world and in history. I argued that such a conception was not to be ruled out as absurd, but that there were difficulties in establishing the grounds on which it could properly be affirmed. I then turned to the fact of Christ, the understanding of his person and the redemptive significance of his death. In that area of the discussion, I stressed two difficulties. The first was the difficulty of historical knowledge, which cannot be by-passed if our affirmations are really intended to be affirmations concerned even in part with the historical figure of Jesus. The second was the difficulty inherent in ascribing universal effects to a particular historical occurrence—as all 'objective' theories of the atonement attempt to do in one way or another. In the course of that discussion I gave some attention to contemporary Christian experience in its claim to be experience of Christ or of the liberating power of his redeeming death. But I was primarily concerned there with the possibility of drawing upon such experience as evidence in support of the once-for-all historical element in traditional christological or atonement doctrines. However, such a reference is never more than one aspect of the experience. Christian experience never understands itself as indicating a special presence or activity of God exclusively in the past. It speaks of such a special presence or activity in the present as well. It does so by describing such experiences as experiences of grace or of the Holy Spirit. On the face of it, this is the most promising area for the kind of investigation on which we are embarked. For there we would be concerned with personal experience, which *prima facie* at least is a more open-textured area than is the natural world. We would also be concerned with the present, and so relieved of some of the taxing historical problems with which we have had to deal. It is this area, therefore, and claims to divine activity of this kind, that I want now to consider.

The experiences with which I am concerned are not, of course, as I have insisted throughout, a kind of pure sense-datum. They arise within an already existing tradition and receive their fundamental shape and interpretation from that tradition. This is already implicit in our description of them as experiences of grace or of the Holy Spirit. Those terms are not absolutely fixed and unalterable in meaning, but they do bring with them a rich texture of meaning from the past. It will be best, therefore, to begin with a brief review of their meaning at the formative roots of the tradition.

The biblical tradition gives clear evidence of the variable nature of the phenomena which may be associated with the Spirit of God. In a number of early Old Testament stories it is closely linked to spectacular occurrences—the extraordinary exploits of a Samson or the ecstatic behaviour of a Saul among the prophets (Judg. 14.6; I Sam. 10.6). In later writings it is more likely to be linked with an understanding of the divine will or with obedience to God's statutes (Ecclus. 39.6; Ezek. 36.26f.). A similar pattern can be traced within the New Testament. The coming of the Spirit at Pentecost is associated with the paranormal phenomenon of the glossolalia and it is that gift of the Spirit which seems most to have impressed the immature Corinthian church. But for Paul it is love which is the first and fullest expression of the Spirit's presence. In both cases it is the strange and inexplicable occurrence which is most readily grasped as evidence of God's spirit at work; but it is phenomena of a very different kind which come to be seen as the religiously most significant examples of that presence. And that same pattern continues. Today also it is most often the abnormal or the unexplained event which prompts people to speak in terms of divine providence or of special grace; but at the reflective level it is likely to be a more generalized conception of God's spirit at work in and through the ordinary occurrences of life which is more valued and more stressed.

What is the significance of such paranormal phenomena? Their place in the biblical tradition and in contemporary experience suggests that even if we are agreed that we ought to play down their religious importance, they might still have an epistemological significance of a kind that is very relevant to our discussion. Are they to be understood as occasions of special divine action? And if so, can that understanding of them as divine action be applied also to what we would call outstanding examples of love or self-sacrifice? Could they be pointers to the reality of divine action in those other areas to which we ascribe greater religious significance but in which we might nevertheless have been unable to detect it with any confidence apart from them? It is very much in this kind of way that Professor Mitchell appears to see them in an essay entitled 'The Grace of God'. For him the appeal to empirical evidence is essentially supplementary, confirmatory of a tradition given in Christian revelation as a whole. Within that context, he sees the more 'spectacular irruptions into the lives of the professedly religious' as providing a clue to the interpretation of a much wider range of human experiences. They are, he writes, 'like the phosphorescent crest of a wave which enables us to detect a sea whose boundaries we could not chart. Having made an entry for the concept of grace by tracing it as it breaks through more or less spectacularly into human experience, we are led on to extend its application to all good works.'[1] This is a powerful image, but how is it to be understood? Paranormal experiences are significant. It is important that in any account we give of the world we should not simply ignore the presence of that which is strange and inexplicable in human experience. But how much does its acknowledgment imply? In what sense, if any, is it rightly to be understood as indicative of divine action, either in itself or in that wider sea which it enables us to detect?

There is certainly a striking similarity between the language natural to the religious interpretation of paranormal experiences and that which is characteristic of cases not involving any features that we would normally regard as paranormal. Someone may describe an experience of conversion as one in which 'God stopped me in my tracks', even when it involves none of the auditory or visual phenomena associated with Paul's experience on the Damascus road. Or people who have undergone a period of great stress may often be heard to say, 'I could never have got through it by my own unaided strength'. What weight should be

[1] Basil Mitchell (ed.), *Faith and Logic*, Allen and Unwin 1957, p.174.

given to such descriptions? Are they anything more than dead metaphors, traditional formulae without serious significance? I do not think they can be taken at their face value; nor, however, do I think they can be dismissed as of no significance whatever. Their weakness and possibly misleading character derives from the basic assumption which seems to underlie them. That assumption is that human behaviour is for most of the time entirely explicable, but that there are a number of experiences that do not fit in this well-understood system, for which some special supplementary explanation needs to be found. But this is a total misrepresentation of the position, a gross failure to recognize the mysterious nature of human behaviour throughout. Human development in every sphere of life is characterized by strange reversals, as inexplicable as any religious conversion. We do not have a fixed quantum of moral or spiritual strength, so we can know in advance how much we could endure unaided and be sure, therefore, when some supernatural help has been forthcoming. We need a general picture of a different kind against which to set men's accounts of the experience of grace if we are to understand the significance of those accounts aright.

It is possible to give an account of human experience of considerable complexity and of considerable coherence without reference to God. Such an account will never be complete. But what is incomplete about it is not a matter of some exceptional phenomena which will not fit into the scheme at all and require some totally different kind of explanation. Some such problem cases no doubt there may be, but they are not the primary reason for the sense of incompleteness in our original account. That incompleteness is one of a much more general kind. A parallel can be drawn with the incompleteness that attaches to a purely physical account of the human body. At one level of treatment that account might attain relative completeness. But however far it progressed at that level, it would always remain radically incomplete in its ability to deal at all with the whole area of psycho-physical interaction and its implications for understanding man's bodily functioning. In a similar way, what is required to fill out a non-theistic account of human life is not some further explanatory agent to account for a number of unexplained phenomena; it is, rather, another explanatory framework from within which to discuss all experience in order to be able to deal with the full range of questions that that experience raises for us.

In the light of these considerations it is questionable whether the special types of experiences, which were the starting-point of this discussion, can rightly be understood as requiring the positing of some special, additional causal factor in the particular situations in question. Even if we are fully justified in speaking of them in terms of grace or of the Holy Spirit, this ought to be seen rather as a reminder of the need for an additional perspective—in this case a religious perspective—from which to view the human scene in general and those experiences in particular. To take the body-mind parallel again. A purely physical account of bodily movements will for some purposes be wholly adequate. Where it is in need of supplementation, what is needed is not the simple inclusion of the human will as an additional factor in an otherwise identical account; what is called for is a separate but related account in terms of the human person as an organic unity, within which a relative but only incomplete separation of the mental and the physical can be made. So in the case of a religious perspective what we have to do is to look at human experience from a standpoint in which God and man are conjoined and in which only a relative and incomplete distinction of their respective roles is possible. And this, surely, is the kind of union of the divine and the human to which grace and the Holy Spirit have always been understood to refer in the main stream of reflective Christian tradition.

Before we go on to work out this broader approach in more detail and to ask whether it provides us with evidence of divine activity of the kind for which we are looking, it is worth recalling how characteristic this move from the more specialized to the more general is, not only in the biblical understanding of the Spirit but in the subsequent history of the doctrine of the Spirit as well. This can be illustrated from the church's understanding of the traditional means of grace—the Bible and the sacraments—and also from the doctrine of the church itself.

In the Nicene creed, the one activity within history directly ascribed to the Holy Spirit is his having 'spoken by the prophets'. In the early centuries there was a tendency to see the role of the human prophet in purely instrumental terms, like the flute in the mouth of the flautist.[2] But such a conception could not hold the field. Two essential modifications (both of which are to be found adumbrated as early as the writings of Origen) became in time a necessary part of any comprehensive account of inspiration. In the first place, it was impossible to sustain a purely passive understanding of the human author's role. The work of the Spirit came to be understood rather in terms of a quickening of the author's natural faculties. Secondly, it was not enough to speak only of the inspiration of the scriptural author. The meaning of Scripture did not lie self-evidently on the surface of the text; nor was its true interpretation simply a matter of human cleverness. The reader also was in need of the

[2] E.g. Athenagoras, *Supplicatio* 9.

special illumination of the Spirit. There had, that is to say, to be a widening of the area of discourse to which the special activity of the Spirit was applied.

Such modifications of the concept of inspiration would be acceptable today to the most conservative of theologians. What they amount to, I want to suggest, is a gradual broadening out of the notion of the Spirit's activity in relation to the inspiration of Scripture. And that process should, I believe, be seen as indicating the need for a shift of perspective of the kind of which I have been speaking. The earliest accounts envisaged the Spirit as a distinct causal factor (indeed the sole truly causal factor) in the production of the scriptural text. This certainly appeared to give a strong sense of the reality and effectiveness of God's action in the world. But it has had to be abandoned. We tend to replace it with a greatly attenuated version of the same basic picture. The Spirit is not so directly the author of the biblical text, but he enhances the natural capacities of the writer, checks his human tendency to error or conveys otherwise inaccessible knowledge about the purposes of God. Ought we not to say that it was a mistake to try to relate the activity of God in that specific way to the production of the biblical text at all? The traditional link between the Holy Spirit and the Bible should rather be understood as expressing the conviction that the biblical writings are of especial importance for man's grasping and responding to God's purpose for the world. It ought not to be understood to involve the need for any additional factor in the story of their emergence.

A similar analysis can be developed in relation to the role of the Spirit in the sacraments as means of grace. Sacramental theology has been riddled with sterile debates about the moment and the nature of the Spirit's coming in baptism and confirmation, at the *epiclesis* or at the words of institution in the eucharist, and in the rite of ordination. The sterility of so much of these debates derives, I would argue, from the same fundamental misconception. And we shall never be free of those debates unless we are prepared to adopt the general shift in perspective which I am here advocating. Traditional theology has hypostatized the Holy Spirit and has tended to ascribe specific activities to him. This has had the laudable intention of emphasizing their profound reality and their personal character. It has, however, had precisely the opposite effect. The more specific the actions ascribed to the Holy Spirit, the more impersonal their understanding becomes. In the theology both of inspiration and of the sacraments, a more personal account has had to go hand in hand with a more generalized account. It is the full implication of that process that needs, I believe, to be more openly recognized.

The history of the doctrine of the church illustrates this characteristic broadening of the horizons in a somewhat different way. In the main body of New Testament thought, the spheres of the Spirit and of the church (so far as it is proper at that stage to speak of the church as a single entity) are coterminous with one another. The church is the eschatological community and the Spirit is the distinctive gift of the eschatological age. The conviction that this is so is grounded both in the promises of Scripture and in the experience of the community, whether dramatically in the speaking with tongues by the apostles at Pentecost and by new converts after baptism, or more generally in the experience of Christ's transforming presence within the community at large. The words of Irenaeus are a fair summary of this central strand of New Testament conviction: 'Where the church is, there is the Spirit of God; and where the Spirit of God is, there is the church and all grace.'[3] But the claimed coincidence of the two spheres was not at all times self-evident. Which, then, was to be seen as determinative of the other? If the promptings of piety favoured the priority of the Spirit, practical considerations pointed in the direction of the church as the determining factor. For Tertullian (at least in his Montanist days) the church is located wherever there is a company of spiritual men; it is *qua* spiritual men that the apostles are the foundation-stone of the church. For Cyprian, on the other hand, it is *qua* bishops that the apostles are the church's foundation-stone. The church is to be recognized by means of the episcopate, and consists of those who are officially in fellowship with that episcopate. There and there only (whatever apparent evidence to the contrary there may be) is the Holy Spirit at work. Neither has modified the underlying conviction of the coincidence of the two spheres; but on the question of how that single coincident sphere of Spirit-church is to be identified, they have moved in diametrically opposed directions.[4] In the continuing conflict of 'sect' and 'church', that same opposition has remained.

Throughout its history the church has always done its best to hold on to that conviction of the coincidence of the two spheres given in its very early traditions. Even when it has taken a positive attitude to the insights and achievements of men right outside the Judaeo-Christian dispensation (and it has generally been more ready to do that than have the sects), it was reluctant to refer such insights or achievements explicitly to the Holy Spirit; even when it was prepared to take a more charitable view of schismatics than Cyprian was, it was inclined still to restrict the work of the Holy Spirit within the confines of the given unity of the

[3] Irenaeus, *Adv. Haer.* 3,24,1.
[4] Cf. R. F. Evans, *One and Holy*, SPCK 1972, pp.33f., 61f.

Catholic Church. But it was only able to be so confident of the exclusive presence of the Spirit's working within the defined limits of the church, either on the basis of explicit promises in Scripture or of a highly triumphalist interpretation of the church's history. The weakness of both lines of argument is too well-known to call for detailed refutation. They have indeed been very largely abandoned. Today Christians are to be found speaking much more freely of the work of the Spirit in the secular world and in other religious faiths. Here too, then, there is a broadening out of the area within which we speak of the operation of the Holy Spirit. In this broader perspective, what we ascribe to the Spirit are those things which we judge to have contributed or to be contributing to the purposes of God for the world. It is that qualitative assessment of them, rather than evidence of anything special about the manner of their occurrence, that is determinative. In the light of this analysis it is by no means obvious that they require to be understood as involving any special form of divine activity in the world.

But in taking the relation between the Spirit and the corporate body of the church as our example of this broadening perspective within which the work of the Spirit has come to be understood, we have not chosen the most promising case for our particular purpose. The operation of the Spirit has with at least equal insistence been claimed for the interior life of the Christian. Can we, by consideration of the ordinary experience of individual Christians, find the kind of evidence for which we are looking? Is there something there which both requires us to speak of God as active and also enables us to do so in a way which is fully coherent with our other beliefs?

The language of personal relationships at the purely human level is extremely difficult to tie down. The more intimate and profound the relationship, the more difficult it is to find the appropriate language to express it. It need hardly surprise us, therefore, that the language of the tradition should be so varied in its attempts to speak of the work of the Holy Spirit at the level of personal experience. The fundamental problem is that of doing justice both to the integrity of personal being and to the all-pervasive nature of that grace which we are seeking to describe. The clash of contrasting approaches finds its classic expression in the conflict between Augustine and Pelagius. At one end of the scale we have the picture of two people standing over against one another, the one offering to the other the help of his advice or of particular forms of practical assistance. Applied to God, the picture emphasizes God's gracious giving of such things as the law to be man's guide and the sacraments to help him on his journey through life. But such a picture fails to deal with the specific area of our present concern. It sees God's help only in the external ordinances of a providential history. Even if deserving of the name of grace and involving some idea of God's action in history, it does not leave room for that internal working in the lives of men which is specifically intended by reference to the Holy Spirit. At the other end of the scale one finds the language of possession. As we have already seen in relation to early conceptions of prophetic inspiration, this may involve an overriding or suspension of the properly personal being of the one possessed. But it need not do so— at least in conscious intention. It and other similar terms have been used to indicate a profound but hidden relationship which is no infringement of personal autonomy but rather an enhancement of truly personal being. Such a conception certainly finds analogy in important human experiences. A man in love may not be able to help himself in responding to the influence of his beloved, and yet may be most fully himself in doing so. Can this picture then be sustained? Does it offer us a viable picture of this way of God's working in the world?

I have already referred to Augustine as the classic exponent of this kind of approach. The greater approval given to Augustine than to Pelagius by most historians of doctrine is not just a re-echoing of the judgment of the church of their day. It is primarily due to Augustine's far more profound apprehension of the issues involved. In the case of human sin, he is surely right in his recognition of the importance of heredity, environment and habit and of the impossibility of treating each individual person or each individual occasion as if it were a *tabula rasa,* with genuinely equal potentiality for right or wrong decision. It is when he attempts to turn this descriptive insight into a causal account of the origins of man's sin that the trouble begins. The resultant account of how man has come to be in this sinful state through Adam's sin and its subsequent transmission to all his descendants has had a disastrous influence and needs to be firmly repudiated. Much the same, it seems to me, is true of his understanding of grace. His account of the intricate functioning of human motivation and of the ways in which the love of God is experienced in the life of the believer shows great depth of spiritual insight and remains of lasting value. But treat it as a causal account of how God works in the world through inner suasions that are effective in this man and not in that, and once again the results are disastrous. There is then no escape, as Augustine himself unwittingly demonstrated, from a doctrine of predestination which strikes at the roots of morality, of true humanity and of belief in a loving God.

It is often argued that the kind of unacceptable conclusion that I have been depicting only follows if grace has been misunderstood as power. Certainly it is when (often from motives of mistaken piety) grace is conceived after the model of an irresistible force that the most disastrous implications arise. And for all his profound insights into the nature of love, Augustine did not wholly free himself from such ideas. Was it then not simply irrelevant or perverse to develop the shortcomings of Augustine's particular analysis, as I have just been doing? If we make this vital correction, if we really eschew all ideas of force in relation to God's working, are we not then left with a viable picture of the way God works in the world through the Holy Spirit? Certainly this was the direction of thought already suggested by the familiar human analogy of the man controlled by love for his beloved. It is a promising line of approach, but it is questionable whether it can do all that is sometimes claimed for it.

Can we then define any more precisely what is implied by speaking of God working by the way of love through the inner promptings of the Holy Spirit? It is certainly not something wholly separable from those other more external gifts such as law and sacramental ordinances. So is it anything more than a way of speaking of the cumulative effect upon us of all those influences for good that by God's providence are available to us in the world? The consensus of tradition and the intuitions of most religious experience provide strong *prima facie* evidence for saying that it is something more than that. But what could this something more be? N. P. Williams claims that 'the ultimate kernel of a "special providence" is a direct influence exerted by God upon the personality of a human being', and goes on to speak of 'deftly administered subconscious impulses'.[5] If

5 N. P. Williams, *The Grace of God*, Longmans 1930, pp.112f.

we are right to look for some kind of causal operation over and above the specifiable external influences, some such language seems difficult to avoid. But would such direct but hidden influence upon the soul be a suasion of love? It is true that in the analogy of human loving we cannot give a full and complete account of the way in which two people in love influence one another. In its organic wholeness there appears to be something more at work than the sum of the various distinguishable elements of which we can become aware. But that something more is not any direct but hidden influence on the soul of an intentional kind. That suggests the way of the indoctrinator, of the hidden persuader rather than the way of love—even if it be intended for the ultimate good of the other. Once again our right and proper concern to speak of something more than we are able to provide through a cumulative account of the various specific forms of help given to us does not seem to require the addition of some further causal factor to the story; treated in that way it has grave, perhaps insuperable, difficulties. It points, rather, to the need for a new and fuller perspective from which to interpret the occurrence as an organic whole. In the case of the human analogy it is not some new specifiable factor at work; it is the spirit of love pervading and transforming all the ordinary means of communication between people that makes the difference. The actual media of communication have not changed. But the change in the whole context within which they are apprehended gives a new feel and a new effectiveness to them. To express this change, new patterns of language are invoked. But care is needed to ensure that that new language is understood to refer to this pervasive change of ethos and not to the addition of some new isolable factor. So in the religious case our talk of the Holy Spirit should perhaps be understood not as suggesting any specific or direct working of God upon the human personality, but rather as a reminder that the love of God is the source of all potentiality for good in the world and that to recognize that fact has a transforming effect upon our apprehension and our realization of that good.

The account that I have given so far will, I fear, appear largely negative and polemical in character. I have been trying to bring out what seem to me to be certain fundamental weaknesses in some traditional conceptions of grace and of the Holy Spirit and in the ways in which it has been felt necessary to interpret them. I have, however, acknowledged all along that those accounts were intended to do justice to religious realities which cannot simply be dismissed as of no substance. Moreover, they do undoubtedly succeed up to a point in conveying that intended sense. But difficulties arise, it seems to me, when we ask the questions that have to be asked about the evidence on which they are grounded and about their coherence with the rest of what we have to say about God and the world. I find myself in a position similar to that which I described in relation to the doctrine of the incarnation. The specific grounds on which the belief appears to be based do not carry full conviction; they do not seem to me to require the doctrine in the way that they have normally been thought to do. Nevertheless, the doctrine might still be true and still demand our assent, if it were required in order for the religious tradition which it has expressed and sustained to have any validity at all.

A claim of this sort is made by Professor Mitchell in the course of the article from which I have already quoted. At that point I quoted simply his argument from the more spectacular aspects of religious experience. It was not, however, an argument on which he himself would want to

place too much weight; he is aware of the danger that it
'may easily convey the impression that grace has only to
do with abnormal, *spectacular* irruptions into the lives of the
professedly religious'.[6] The lives of the saints are for him a
more worthwhile, even if more difficult, court of appeal.
The essence of his argument is:

The concept of saintliness as we receive it from our common Christian
tradition is closely bound up with the notion of God-dependence and
cannot be detached from it without radical change of meaning . . .
We cannot regard saintliness as a purely natural flowering of the
human spirit without affirming that it contains as part of its essence
the capacity to be fundamentally deluded. For the saint's life is charac-
teristically centred upon God. A man can be a poet without caring a
fig for poetic inspiration. He can scarcely be a saint without recognizing his dependence upon God.[7]

In other words, Professor Mitchell claims that we are forced
to choose between accepting the saint's conviction about
the pervasive working of God's grace in his life on the one
hand and dismissing the whole tradition of Christian saintliness as a form of self-delusion on the other.

But we have to ask what is meant by God-dependence.
What does the notion necessarily involve? This line of
argument is pursued in more detail and with diametrically
opposed conclusions by Professor Maclagan in his *Theological Frontier of Ethics*. He insists that 'for a theist a doctrine
of grace in some form is *analytically* involved in his basic
belief'.[8] but then goes on to consider whether empirical
evidence can indicate what form that doctrine ought to
take. With this end in view he turns his attention to the

⁶ Op. cit., p.174.
⁷ Ibid., pp.172f.
⁸ W. G. Maclagan, *The Theological Frontier of Ethics*, Allen and Unwin
1961, p.149.

practice of prayer and in particular the prayer of the believer that his 'will itself may be "conformed" to God's will and "enabled" '.[9] Here is the essence of saintliness in its most characteristic form of self-expression. Are we then forced to choose between accepting the validity of its self-understanding on the one hand and treating it as a sheer delusion on the other? Maclagan finds a middle path between the two by insisting that taking the language of prayer seriously does not involve taking it literally. He cites the analogy of the prayer for forgiveness of sin. This, he argues, though petitionary in outward form, needs ultimately to be understood not as a request for something to be granted contingently upon our prayer but as a way of expressing the contrition which is the appropriate spiritual response to the recognition of our past sin. Similarly, he concludes, 'what appears as petition for grace to make the resolution required of us is in fact the moral victory, itself the resolution for which it seems to ask'.[10]

I believe that this type of analysis may point the way out of the dilemma with which we seemed to be faced. It suggests the sort of way in which it may be possible to provide an account which would do justice to the religious realities that underlay teaching about grace, even of an Augustinian kind, but which would at the same time be free of its attendant difficulties. In outline form the account would go something like this. Man has been created with a capacity for awareness of God and of an ultimate divine purpose for the world. This capacity can become actual through general reflection on the world in which we live. But it is not in fact realized equally and uniformly in all the varied conditions of human existence. Some aspects of human experience give rise to it more frequently and more

---

[9] Ibid., p.157.   [10] Ibid., p.164.

profoundly than others. In the experience of our culture, the records of the Christ event and occasions of worship which focus on that event are particularly powerful agents in giving rise to such awareness. It may flood in upon a person with unexpected suddenness, or it may arise gradually as the outcome of much labour, thought and meditation. My description so far probably sounds highly intellectualist in character; this is a difficulty, never easily overcome in theological discussion. But it should be evident from what was said in my earlier discussion of belief in God in general that such awareness is never a purely external, uninvolved type of awareness. Since it is an awareness which concerns the ultimate character of the world as a whole, it necessarily includes awareness of my own place in and my own relation to the whole. It cannot by its very nature leave me unaffected. It has the power to affect my attitudes and my actions at the deepest level of my being. The particular kinds of attitude or action to which it gives rise cannot be prescribed in detail in advance. They will be in part dependent on the particular changing circumstances in which I happen to be. They will be the outcome of an interaction between those contingent circumstances and the larger concept of an eternal divine purpose (itself, of course, only imperfectly glimpsed from the restricted standpoint of my own situation).

These, I want to suggest, are the characteristics of religious experience that give rise to talk about grace and about the Holy Spirit. The limits of human experience cannot be fully defined or predicted. Man's imaginative and active faculties can be expanded by the vision of God in ways that continue to excite and to surprise us. It is these features which justify the kind of language that is to be found both in the tradition and on the lips of ordinary religious people. But when we speak of particular occasions—whether the inspiration of Scripture, a eucharistic service, the history of the church, the lives of the saints or even special experiences of our own —as scenes of the Holy Spirit's activity, we need not (indeed I would be bold enough to say we ought not) imply thereby that they are occasions in which some special supernatural causation is to be looked for. Such a description should rather, I suggest, be understood to mean that here are places where the purpose of God has been apprehended, expressed or put into effect in a particularly profound way. In other words, language about the Holy Spirit is language designed to describe the occasions in which the divine purpose finds effective realization in human life.

6

FINAL REFLECTIONS

I have entitled this book *The Remaking of Christian Doctrine*. That it has been concerned with doctrine and that it proposes a measure of change will, I think, be evident enough. I have tried to set out some of the main grounds for questioning certain aspects of traditional Christian doctrine and to suggest in the barest outline the direction in which doctrinal construction might be undertaken. It has been a deliberately bare sketch that I have given. I have introduced none of the distinctive vocabulary which characterizes the work of so many constructive theologians of our own time. There have been, as far as I am aware, no neologisms of the kind that figure in the writings of a Tillich or a Teilhard, of a Rahner or a Lonergan. I realize that this is primarily because I could not, even had I attempted to do so, have begun to emulate either the philosophical competence or the intellectual range of such theological giants. But I want to claim the merits of my defects. It means, I hope, that both the points of tension with the past and also the general direction of change envisaged have stood out with reasonable clarity.

What will perhaps have appeared less self-evident to some is whether the doctrine envisaged is genuinely *Christian* doctrine and whether the kind of changes advocated constitute a *remaking* rather than an unmaking. If I am to establish this with the same degree of clarity, more discussion is called for. As I said at the outset, my appeal to the principles of 'economy' and 'coherence' seems to me at least to be something distinguishable from the methods of so-called 'reductionism' and 'rationalism'. In this final chapter, therefore, I want to review the emerging pattern of doctrine more carefully as a whole and to try to justify my claim that it does constitute a viable form of that necessarily continuous process of remaking by which alone Christian doctrine can flourish as a living and constructive activity.

In the first chapter I gave some attention to the question of development, of the relation of any contemporary Christian doctrine to its past. I was primarily concerned there to stress the unpredictability of the extent and direction of change and the impossibility of laying down any fixed criteria for determining what should or should not be acceptable. The element of continuing identity would, I suggested, 'have to be looked for in the sources to which reference is made, the kinds of concern which direct that reference and the general pattern or character of the affirmations made'.[1] How do my own suggestions look in the light of these rough guides?

On the first two counts no serious objection can, I think, be raised. I have drawn throughout on the witness of Scripture and on the history of the Christian tradition. It is true that I have seldom quoted explicit texts of Scripture or specific conciliar decisions. But doing so is only one way of referring to those sources, and in the light of our contemporary understanding of their nature and of their variety it is a way that is liable to be misleading. It can very easily be taken to imply a falsely authoritarian view of their role; it does not necessarily do so, but the extent to which it has

[1] See p.7 above.

been used like that in the past renders it still liable to such misunderstanding. My avoidance of it does not imply any abandonment of a serious reference to those Christian sources. I do not think that on this point my approach is anything unusual for a theologian who has reflected at all deeply on the implications of critical historical study in the realms of Scripture and church history.

Nor do I think that there is anything unusual in the 'kinds of concern' which have directed that reference. It might be objected that those concerns have been too narrowly intellectual in character. I do not think, however, that that objection can be sustained. I have continually insisted that the evidence of our sources must be interpreted in a way that makes some sort of positive sense of the religious tradition. Our interpretation must be one that offers not only a tenable philosophical world-view but also a faith to be lived by. If that should prove impossible, then indeed one would have not a remaking of Christian doctrine but its cessation. If that more directly religious concern has appeared at times somewhat minimal or unduly muted, that will (I hope) be rectified by what I have to say later in this chapter.

The real difficulty relates to the third point: 'the general pattern or character of the affirmations made'. I have acknowledged throughout that the affirmations I have been making have, in very general terms, a non-incarnational pattern or character to them. Can we assess both whether this is a right pattern in the light of all the evidence and also whether it involves too drastic a change of general character to be acceptable as something held within a continuing sense of identity?

Before embarking on the main line of discussion, it is important to recall briefly the overall context within which that discussion is being conducted. In the first place, while acknowledging the substantial degree of doctrinal change here envisaged, I would argue that this has to be seen against an understanding of the history of doctrine as one of continuous change. Traditional accounts, while accepting the reality of change in the past, tend to underestimate the extent and the fundamental nature of it. How does our faith compare with that of a Tertullian, for whom the basic character of Christian existence was to belong to a small group, living in the extreme end of time, in self-conscious separation from a world about to perish? And what of Augustine, for whom the goal of the whole dramatic scheme of salvation was the preservation of a fixed number of the elect to make up the number of the fallen angels? And what of Gregory the Great, for whom God had communicated to men through the elaborate allegories of the scriptural record whose human authors were no more than a pen in the hand of their real divine author? The differences between their forms of faith and those which most of us hold today are not peripheral. They affect the whole conception of the nature of the Christian God and of his relation to the world. It is against the background of changes of this order of magnitude that any evaluation of the kind of change that I am proposing needs to be set.

And even if the changes now proposed should still appear more substantial than parallel changes in the past, that ought not to be any occasion for surprise. The cultural changes which have been the primary reason for doctrinal change in the past impinge on us today with greatly increased intensity and speed. At the end of his recent study of the doctrine of the church in Latin patristic thought, which includes studies of Tertullian, of Augustine and of Gregory the Great, R. F. Evans reflects in these terms:

Certainly the cultural shifts occurring in the period stretching from the end of the second century to the beginning of the seventh were less marked than the cultural distance which separates us from that entire period; yet precisely in the earlier period we do find occurring the marked changes of thought which the preceding chapters have pointed out. . . . The astonishing thing about the fathers is the resolution with which they introduce and rationalize novelty in spite of what we would call their frequently unhistorical assumptions concerning the unchanging character of Christian truth.[2]

Novelty, then, there has always been; but novelty of a still more far-reaching kind in our own day with the increased pace of cultural change is something for which we ought not merely to be prepared, but which we ought positively to expect.

The increased intensity and speed of cultural change which lies behind the kinds of change that I have been advocating can be seen also in the changes of understanding that characterize almost every aspect of human knowledge today. We ought not to expect theological knowledge to be exempt from its effects. Its exact character can be analysed in various ways. I would like to emphasize three factors: a more empirical approach to knowledge; a changed attitude to the role of authority; and a changed understanding of the accessibility of the past. I am sure that these changes are real changes and have to be taken seriously. Whether their implications have been rightly construed in the argument of the preceding pages is another question, and one that can only be answered through the cut and thrust of continuing debate. What I shall attempt to do in the remainder of this chapter is to review my conclusions in the light of two very general questions:

1. Do they achieve their intended goals of economy and coherence?

[2] R. F. Evans, *One and Holy*, p.161.

2. Is the essential religious concern preserved? Do they provide (as doctrine must do) the framework of a faith to be lived?

First, then, how far have I achieved my aims of economy and coherence? Neither aim can be pushed to the limit. If an explanatory account were determined to do without everything that was not directly or irrefutably given in experience, it would certainly cease to explain, even if it did not also cease to exist. If an explanatory account were perfectly coherent, it would cease to be true. Life is too untidy for that; it reveals order, but not perfect order.

God is not directly and irrefutably given. It is not only the fool who says there is no God. You can be an atheist without being a fool; lots of people are. But when the principle of economy beckons me to dispense with the concept of God, I resist. To do so would be to leave a whole dimension of human experience even more opaque and inexplicable than it already is. Yet if it is true that any faithful account of human experience is bound to lack absolute coherence, an account which incorporates the concept of God is sure to lack it even more blatantly. The infinite God is infinitely resistant to our finite systematizations.[3]

The prophet who declares the word of the Lord and the saint who lives in an immediate awareness of God's presence are not worried by such things. Their language abounds in paradox which the reflective religious mind finds strangely puzzling and convincing at the same time. Good theology does not try to eliminate this element of paradox or incoherence altogether. It could not do so, I have been arguing, without ceasing to be theology, without ceasing to talk about God altogether—and even then it could not succeed

[3] See pp.33–4 above.

in doing so without remainder. It tends, rather, to impose some sort of shape or order on the unsystematic utterances of saint and prophet by fixing the point at which the element of absurdity or incoherence is most appropriately to be located. If this is in danger of taming them, of evacuating them of their religious power, it is nonetheless a necessary part, the rational part, of a fully human response to them. Perhaps one of the most important distinctions between the Western and the Eastern theological traditions is to be found in the different point at which each has chosen to locate the crux of incoherence in relating God to the world. The West places it between God and the world. God is pure actuality; in him is no potency, nothing more waiting to be realized; complete in himself, he is in need of nothing for his own self-fulfilment. How, then, is it that he creates? Can his relation to his creation be a real relation in himself? Can he give himself to his creation, or is the 'created grace' that he bestows something supernatural but less than himself? The tradition has, of course, its answers to these questions, but they are the points of essential incoherence, the points of embarrassment to the theologian, however much the religious man may take them in his stride. The Eastern tradition is different. The religious ideal of divinization will allow of no such qualifications in the account of God's self-giving to man in grace. The point of incoherence is pushed right back into the being of God himself. The point of ultimate paradox is the distinction of the divine essence and the divine energies. Both are uncreated, both are fully divine; there is a distinction but not a division between them; they are not two parts of God, but two modes of his existence in the one of which he is utterly unknowable, in the other of which he is infinitely giveable to man. 'The divine nature,' says Lossky, 'must be called at the same time incommunicable and in a sense communicable; we attain participation in the nature of God, and yet he remains totally inaccessible. We must preserve both things at once and must preserve the antinomy as the criterion of piety.'[4] It is there, at the heart of the divine being, that the East locates the inescapable point of incoherence.

If I may return from such flights to a rather homely simile, the work of theology sometimes seems to me rather like trying to smooth out the bulges when laying a carpet. As soon as you have achieved your immediate aim of getting rid of them at one point, you find that they have reappeared in much the same form somewhere else. It is instructive to observe how often theologians in the West, reacting against the element of incoherence in the traditional Western account of God's relation with the world, come up themselves with something similar to the Eastern tradition—at least in this point of basic structure. The element of incoherence that they have sought to remove from the account of God's relation with the world reappears in their account of God himself. In the theology of Karl Barth there is no essential problem about God's self-giving to man, for God is both 'One who rules and commands in majesty and One who obeys in humility . . . the one and the other without any cleft or differentiation'.[5] For the process theologian there is no essential problem about the transcendent God's activity in the world, for God is dually transcendent and there is distinction (but not division) between his primordial and his consequent natures. In both cases, as for the Eastern tradition, the antinomy, the point of ultimate incoherence, is thrown back into the being of God himself.

[4] Vladimir Lossky, *The Vision of God*, Faith Press 1963, p.127.
[5] Karl Barth, *Church Dogmatics* IV, 1, T. & T. Clark 1956, p.202.

Reflection of this kind upon the history of the tradition as a whole has made me reluctant to identify myself strongly with any one form of the tradition rather than another. Each has its point of incoherence, as it is bound to do. None seems to me to be overall superior to the other when judged by the criterion of coherence. Each has its points of strength and its points of weakness. Each, if used critically, can rightly be used to illuminate differing aspects of our experience. But for that very reason, each needs to be extremely restrained in the kind of claims that it makes for its own particular vision.

Such an apparently accommodating attitude to varying traditions in relation to the doctrine of God may seem to stand in somewhat striking contrast to the more strongly critical stance I have been advocating in relation to incarnational doctrine. Am I guilty of operating a double standard? Have I been applying my aims of economy and coherence in that sphere with an inconsistently greater degree of rigour? I fully acknowledge the force of the objection. It certainly seems to be true in my experience that many of those Christian philosophers who are most acutely aware of the intellectual difficulties inherent in the basic affirmations of theism are almost naively credulous in their handling of the historical traditions about Jesus, while many of those who are most scrupulously critical in their assessment of those historical traditions seem unwarrantably easy-going in the confidence with which they continue to affirm their basic theistic convictions. Criticism in the sphere in which one is expert frequently finds its compensation in a much less critical attitude in the area of someone else's expertise. It is a fault more easily detected in others than in oneself, and the possibility that it is true in one's own case has to be taken very seriously.

The objection might perhaps be developed in some such terms as these. You have acknowledged, it might be said, the difficulty and inconclusiveness of all arguments for the existence of God. Yet you continue to affirm a form of theistic belief on the ground that our experience as a whole justifies, and for you at least requires, some such conviction. There is nothing at all remarkable, of course, in that, for it has been the stock-in-trade of theistic thinkers for many generations. You indeed, it might be added, have tended to go further than most and have seen in the absence of formal argument some justification for an eclectic drawing upon a whole range of differing theistic traditions. But then you have gone on to claim a similar kind of difficulty and inconclusiveness in all the varied arguments for a unique incarnation of God in the person of Jesus. Some, no doubt, will challenge the validity of the criticisms you raise against the conclusiveness of those arguments. But even if it be allowed, what is its force? To show up the fallacy of the arguments does no more to dispose of the doctrine than it does in the case of theism as a whole.

To put the question in this way is eminently fair; what would not be fair would be to imply that once it has been raised in this way, only one answer is conceivable. One has to go on to ask, as in the case of theism, whether Christian experience as a whole does or does not still seem to justify, or even to require, explicit incarnational affirmations. I have tried all along to stress the importance of putting the problem in this form as well as in terms of the validity of more particularized arguments. Perhaps such an issue can only be determined by a consensus of Christian reflection over a considerable period of time after the issue has been explicitly raised. The most that I can do here is to outline the considerations which tend to point me on this issue in a direction different from that which I have followed in relation to the basic issue of theism.

The most obvious distinction between general theistic belief and belief in a specific incarnation in the person of Jesus is this. Belief in God as creator or God as the source of grace are beliefs about something which is continuous or, at least, about something of which there are (if the belief be true at all) many present instances. Belief in God as incarnate in Jesus, even if in some sense true all the time, is in its primary sense true only of a particular time in past history. Thus even if both types of belief have their inevitable element of incoherence, and the criteria for determining whether and in what sense they can properly be held are equally elusive in both cases, there is an additional element of indirectness in any assessment of incarnational belief. It is possible for us to have first-hand experience of what it is to be created beings or to be the recipients of grace (however difficult it may be to know quite what to make of those experiences); in no sense can we have first-hand experience of what it is to be incarnate. The point must not be over-stressed. We are certainly not restricted to belief in things we can experience, and therefore test, at first hand. Some beliefs, though not immediately related to what we experience, may be the necessary precondition of our having the experiences we do have at all. But it does not seem to be true that belief in the incarnation stands in this kind of relation to the experiences of creatureliness or of grace. It is undoubtedly true that it does affect the precise form that they will take. But the presence of such experiences in other, non-incarnational religions is strong evidence against any claim that the belief is necessary for the having of such experiences at all. The two types of belief do not therefore seem to be logically interdependent in the strong sense that they stand or fall together absolutely. And in the process of trying to assess the truth of religious beliefs as we have to do it today, there is a certain initial advantage in the case of beliefs which relate in the more direct way to our experience.

The point is well illustrated by a challenge brought by Professor Cunliffe-Jones against Professor Lampe's essay in the recent Cambridge christology symposium.[6] He fully accepts the difficulties which Professor Lampe there raised about a Logos/Son christology of a traditional type, namely 'that it almost inevitably leads to a diminution of either Christ's humanity or his deity' (p.120). But he goes on to ask whether Professor Lampe's suggested Spirit-christology, with its use of the category of 'Spirit-possession', fares any better. He crystallizes his argument in these words: 'So far as I can see, Indwelling and Incarnation—though very different conceptions—belong in the same area of discourse. If we accept that God, through Christ, indwells his people without disrupting their integrity, this seems to me a real pointer towards the affirmation that God was, in fact, incarnate in Christ, without disrupting his human integrity.' He asks not for any less critical an appraisal of the concept of incarnation, but for a more critical treatment of the concept of indwelling. That is something which I aimed to provide in the previous chapter. The difficulties of the conception, as I tried to show then, are very real. But I do not think that the two distinguishable concepts stand or fall together. The fact that we are in a position to experience that to which 'indwelling' is intended to refer places it in a different position for us when it comes to a critical appraisal

[6] In a privately circulated paper, quoted here with Professor Cunliffe-Jones' kind permission. Professor Lampe's essay, 'The Holy Spirit and the Person of Christ', is in S. W. Sykes and J. P. Clayton (eds.), *Christ, Faith and History*, pp.111–30.

of its inherent difficulties from that of the concept of a single and unique incarnation.

But a position, though more difficult to establish than another, may yet end up equally well established. The fact that a line of argument has to be indirect does not mean that it is bound to be inconclusive. It just means that the road will be longer and there will be more traps for the unwary along the way. As one stage along the road of trying to assess the claim of incarnational belief on our assent, I want now to take up my second question: Does the position which I have been outlining (and in particular its questioning of the idea of a specific unique incarnation) provide the framework for a living faith?

It is sometimes argued that Christian belief is impaled inescapably on the horns of a dilemma. It can either be stated in a strong form, in which it is interesting but almost sure to be false. Or it can be stated in a weak form, in which it has some chance of being true but ceases to be interesting. A robust incarnational faith which speaks of a God who has lived a human life and died a human death; that would be a faith which had bite to it, a faith worth believing—if one could. But hedge and qualify that understanding of incarnation and the faith will die, if not of the thousand qualifications themselves, then of the boredom of its own attenuated claims. Many Christians will readily accept the analysis implicit in this objection—they differ only in their conviction that the faith is in fact true in its strong and robust sense.

But ought we to accept this dichotomy so easily? It is characteristic of all positions that the more extreme their presentation, the more interesting they appear. The political extremist, be he of the right or of the left, is usually more interesting and more quickly able to attract response than the man of the middle. But it is often a superficial kind of interest and the immediate attractiveness of such positions does not necessarily win for them our more considered approval. It is the truth of the matter that concerns us. And if the middle position seems to us to be most true, we do not blame it for its less exciting, and more attenuated appearance. We may regret the difficulty in making it more appealing and more attractive, but we do not criticize it or abandon it for that reason. We keep our criticism for the superficiality with which men so often make their judgments, and we redouble our efforts to present the truth we have seen in as lively a form as we are able without distortion.

But we do not need to turn to political parallels. We can observe the same phenomenon within Christian history. Let us take two obvious examples. A doctrine of revelation such as I described just now as characterizing the thought of Gregory the Great has an immediate appeal. It affirms a direct and utterly reliable communication of God to men in the dictated words of Scripture. It affirms a secure, revealed knowledge of God not otherwise accessible to man. Beside it, most contemporary accounts of revelation wear an attenuated air. For the great majority of people they are less easy to grasp; they do not provide the same degree of assurance or security. Nevertheless, the reflective religious mind does not dismiss them as uninteresting or untrue. It sees in them not merely a reduced or rationalistic account of revelation, reluctantly accepted because the real and robust doctrine is no longer tenable; it sees in them a religiously more profound account of God's dealings with mankind, one in which the freedom of a fully human response is taken with full seriousness.

A similar story can be told in the case of the relation

between theology and ethics. It is sometimes claimed that Christian belief can only have significant ethical implications if that belief takes the form of a deontological ethic, in which the sole criterion of right action would be obedience to the revealed will of God. Such a belief would clearly have an immediate force. Yet our objection to it is not only that it is false, but that it would be morally disastrous. It does not, however, follow from this that Christian belief has no ethical corollaries. Every moral position has implicit within it some overall philosophical viewpoint, some judgment about what things are of real worth in the world. Christianity offers a fundamental perspective of that kind and a community within which its implications can be felt and can be worked out. The whole business has an indirectness and a complexity about it that pose problems of which the older deontological scheme was free. But the faith so understood remains one with important ethical implications; indeed, it becomes one in which moral judgment and moral action can flourish in a fuller and more genuinely personal way.

The point that I am trying to make is that religious positions have often come to be held in a less direct or absolutist form. In general their relation to the life of faith in their revised form is more complex to grasp and less readily assimilated. But it does not cease to exist, and may well prove to be more profoundly personal in character. So it may also prove to be in the case of incarnational belief. It would be absurd to lay down in advance a blueprint of all the conditions to be met if a faith is in fact to be a living faith. The pattern of belief that I have been trying to develop is belief in God upon whom the world depends for its very existence, a God who cares about human suffering, who has a purpose for the world which men can come in part at least to know, and who elicits from men a mature response of faith and love in which sin can begin to be overcome and the goals of human life begin to be realized. Moreover, the central figure within history who focuses for us the recognition and the realization of these things is Jesus Christ. In Christian history all this has undoubtedly been held together and vividly expressed by the doctrine of the unique incarnation of God in Jesus Christ. I have been arguing that that particular doctrine is not required for the whole pattern of belief to be true, or indeed for our having good grounds for believing it to be true.

Let me try to test this claim in relation to John Baker's book, *The Foolishness of God*, to which I have referred before as a sensitive recent statement of the case for a full incarnational belief. In the course of his discussion he describes both negatively and positively the sort of difference which the exclusion or incorporation of an explicitly incarnational belief would make to Christian theism. Negatively he makes his point in this way. Denial of the incarnation would imply the conception of a God who could say: 'If men are to be free to find their true fulfilment, they must know the truth about their eternal situation. This truth can only be given to them in a personal existence, a human being who will be morally comprehensible to them. But this life will involve the most terrible suffering. *I will therefore send someone else to do the job.*'[7] But this line of argument (as Mr Baker himself implicitly recognizes in the way in which he continues his discussion) simply will not do. It assumes that the concept of God incarnate is an intelligible option which is then rejected in favour of some other (less demanding) alternative. But that is not the issue at all. God, it is accepted, makes himself known and available to man in love in the fullest way that is compatible with man's existence as a free

[7] John Austin Baker, *The Foolishness of God*, p.308.

being. What that is, is precisely the issue at stake. And that can only be discovered (if it can be discovered at all) by reflection on the world as it impinges on us. Positively, John Baker describes the significance of incarnational belief over and above a more general theistic belief in these impressive words:

When above all we learn that God himself has become our partner and our brother, sharing our own condition, this gives imperishable glory to every created thing. Never again can we despise or hate the earth trodden by the feet of God, the food and drink by which he lived, the family bonds which he shared, the human form which was found sufficient to express even his innermost being.[8]

That is finely said; but in terms of substance it adds nothing to what is already given in belief in God's creative role and his purpose for the world. The glory of the created order, the potential for good of the natural setting of our human life, the worth of human relationships—all these are implicit in the kind of theistic belief that I have been developing. They do not logically require belief in the incarnation.

If that be true, then the approach that I have been following cannot, I believe, justly be accused of failing to provide the framework of a living faith. But more than a framework is required. In the political parallel that I was developing a little while ago, I said that if one was convinced of the truth of a middle way but recognized its lack of attractive power as compared with more extreme positions, the task that was then incumbent upon one would be to express that position in as lively a form as was possible without distortion. So with theology. The goal that I have been setting myself in this book is one particular goal within the whole compass of theological activity. My aims of economy and coherence have been designed to lay bare a basic, coherent framework

[8] Op. cit., p.313.

of what the Christian evidence seems to require of us. But I have always stressed that such an approach does not exhaust the whole range of theological work. To do only what is required of us is proverbially the mark of the unprofitable servant. The mysterious nature of the reality which we are seeking to interpret means that, having clarified as best we can the basic framework within which we have to work, there is further work of a more tentative kind still to be done. In dialectical relationship with the drive for economy and coherence must go a bold and creative use of the speculative imagination. Without that, no theology, however impeccable its intellectual credentials, will provide the substance of a living faith.

How, then, is the theologian to proceed at this point? However creative he may wish—indeed may have a duty—to be, he cannot simply invent the appropriate images or weave them out of his own private imagination. He must draw upon the images available to him in the tradition in which he stands. And within the Christian tradition those images are inextricably interwoven with incarnational belief. The theologian thus finds himself in a difficult position. If he continues to draw upon that imagery, he will find himself accused of living on borrowed capital or of seeking to hold on to the benefits of a belief that he no longer holds. But the substance of what has been said so far should provide him with the arguments needed to justify a plea of not guilty to that charge, however incriminating the circumstances may appear to others. If, on the other hand, he simply abandons the use of all such language, he is likely to give an equally false impression. He will appear to many to identify himself with a simple negation of all that was implicit in the old view, as the example drawn from John Baker's book suggests. But the shift in understanding is nothing like as straightforward as that. It is a far more subtle change in conceptuality with which we have to do.

There is, then, no call upon the theologian to abandon all the old imagery. It is indeed incumbent upon him to continue to draw upon it, for it contains within itself the only available resources of meaning to express vividly the very realities that he desires to express. He may do so with the fullest integrity, provided the understanding of that imagery is all the time being modified by its interaction with critical questioning of the kind that I have been trying to pursue here. What the ultimate outcome of such an inter-action will be, it is idle to speculate. Our task is to map out the way in which we should proceed now and not to legislate for the distant future.

We speak of the world as God's handiwork. Our know-ledge of the evolutionary development of the world means that when we spell out that belief in detail we are bound to do so in ways very different from our forefathers. But that does not evacuate the conviction of its religious importance; nor does it destroy the underlying reality of the world's ontological dependence upon God which is the ultimate basis of such pictorial language. We speak of certain events in history as acts of God. Our approach to the understand-ing of world history means that when we spell out that belief in detail we are most likely to do so in ways very dif-ferent from our forefathers. But that does not evacuate the language of all religious meaning, or undermine the truth that there are particular events which have embodied and forwarded the purposes of God for the world of his creation. We speak of God's presence and God's power in the experi-ence of grace. Our approach to the understanding of human personality and of human motivation means that when we spell out that belief in more detail we may well be led to do so in ways very different from our forefathers. But that does nothing to detract from the profound importance of those occasions when a man acknowledges and responds with his full self to all that he has come to know of God and of God's purposes for good; nor does it diminish the transforming power that such experiences can have on all the rest of his life. We speak of God's unique, incarnate presence in the life of Jesus. Within the unity provided by a hallowed formula, this has already been understood in a variety of very different ways down the ages. The reflections that I have been trying to share lead me to the conclusion that here too our spelling out of that conviction will be increasingly different—moving, it may be, altogether outside the possible bounds of the ancient hallowed formulae. But even here there will be a continuity of religious reality in the conviction that it is supremely through Jesus that the character of these purposes of God and the possibility of this experience of grace has been grasped and made effective in the world. If we speak of him as unique and of his claims as universal, the appropriate meaning to be given to such affirmations would seem to be two-fold. They bear witness to the radical nature of the transforming effect in the lives of those who have responded to him; and they express the conviction (which only time can test) that he will continue to fulfil that role in the future, however different the conditions of life may become.

Now if this is the general pattern in which Christian doctrine is to be remade, there is plenty of continuing work to be done. But there will be some questions (particularly in the sphere of christological belief) that have been in the past and still are a cause of grave anxiety to the Christian theologian which he will no longer need to pursue. He will come to see them as questions which cannot be answered and which (despite what has often been assumed in the past) do not need to be answered in order to safeguard the religious realities of Christian faith. If that seems a somewhat negative outcome of this whole enterprise, it constitutes (if true) not only a freedom from certain inevitably fruitless and frustrating lines of enquiry; it constitutes also a freedom for a less restricted and potentially more creative pursuit of the real questions.

THE RESURRECTION
OF THE BODY

All belief about God is problematic. For in our beliefs about
God we are reaching out to speak of a realm beyond the
level of our ordinary experiencing. Little wonder that men
have often declared that such knowledge is only possible if
God has in some direct and supernatural way disclosed to
us truths about his being and his purposes! Much the same
is true of belief about the future. Such beliefs have an in-
security, a tentativeness about them, different in kind from
the uncertainty which also attends our reconstructions of
the past. Small wonder again that men should have given
their attention to prophets and astrologers who have
claimed some more direct vision or foreknowledge of the
future! The area of belief which I want to consider in this
paper combines the difficulties of both. Christian hope is
concerned with God and with the future. If we abandon the
idea of any direct supernatural disclosure in either sphere,
can we continue to give expression to beliefs about this
aspect of Christian faith which will have both a sound basis
and an intelligible content? And if we can, what is the most
appropriate form of such beliefs?

It would be false to suggest that the traditional understanding of Christian hope has been grounded exclusively
on alleged divine disclosures or on predictive prophecy.

God is sovereign and free, but not in the sense of being un-predictable. He is the same, yesterday, today and for ever. Knowledge of what God has done and is doing can there-fore be claimed to include in some measure knowledge of what God will do. Eternal life is spoken of in Scripture and in Christian tradition not simply as a future hope but as a present experience. In other words, traditional Christian beliefs about the future have always had at least an impor-tant part of their grounding in past and present experience. They are not of such a kind that they have to be ruled out in advance on the ground that they could only exist at all on the basis of unacceptable epistemological foundations.

In popular thought today, Christian hope is very largely identified with belief in individual survival of death. This has not always been the case. In the very earliest stage of Chris-tian history, reflected in the New Testament, the funda-mental form of the hope was the expected *parousia* and God's consummation of all things. But that hope always incor-porated a resurrection of those who would have died before it, and the numbers of those so affected grew steadily. Thus it is not unreasonable to take the idea of personal life after death as the central point of our enquiry, provided we recognize that it needs to be set in a wider context than the customary connotation of the phrase is liable to suggest.

The most familiar form of this basic Christian conviction is the credal affirmation of faith in 'the resurrection of the body'. To many, the continued use of that phrase is a clear example of the archaizing tendency of the church to retain her old language and her old concepts, however inappro-priate. But in much *theological* writing, the early church is warmly commended for preferring the resurrection of the body to the immortality of the soul as the way of expressing its belief in a life beyond death. That preference, it is claimed, is of continuing importance for Christian belief today. 'Our modern theology and philosophy,' wrote Oliver Quick, 'have hardly perceived either the width of the gulf which separates a belief in resurrection from a belief in mere immortality, or by what providential guidance the Church was enabled from the first to stand firmly on the side of resurrection.'[1] Since he wrote those words nearly fifty years ago, there has been a good deal of writing, both theological and philosophical, designed to do just that—to stress the gulf between the two concepts and the wisdom of the church's preference for the latter.

It is to this contention in particular that I want to address myself. What is the real nature of the difference between these two forms of expression? Is the difference between them as clear and the superiority of the concept of resurrection as marked as is so often claimed? But the discussion of that issue cannot be kept wholly separate from discussion of the wider issue of the grounds for any form of belief in life after death at all. The most appropriate formulation of a belief cannot be wholly divorced from the reasons for holding it.

I propose to begin by looking simply at the concept of resurrection—with the implicit or explicit contrast with immortality in mind—and to leave the concept of body (and its contrast with soul) to the second half of the paper.

Let us, therefore, begin with the claim that resurrection language does better justice to the fact that God is source, and sole possible source, of any life after death. The argument goes something like this. Man, as the realism alike of the Old Testament and of the modern world knows well, is 'like unto the beasts that perish'. When you are dead, you are dead. That is a fundamental fact about human life, and

[1] Oliver C. Quick, *The Christian Sacraments*, p.94.

the Christian must not seek to soften or to evade it. Any belief in life after death which is rooted in the nature of man as he is is nothing more than self-deception. A future life can only be understood as a new act of God, a new act of creation as gratuitous and uncaused as the original creative act itself. Thus the realism which takes death seriously, and the religious insight which ascribes all to the sheer grace of God, combine to insist that the only possible form of life after death is a resurrected life, something given anew by the creative act of God. The passage quoted from Oliver Quick continues with the words: 'The inherent difference between the two doctrines seems to be this. Resurrection as such implies restoration of life after death and possibly through death: immortality as such implies persistence of life as untouched by death.'

This line of argument is not without force, but it involves a number of strands and calls for careful analysis. Any claim that only resurrection language can do justice to the idea of life after death as God-given is falsely conceived. A comparison with the doctrine of creation may help to make the point clear. At times it has been claimed that for man to be in the fullest sense the creation of God, we must postulate a special act of divine creation at the emergence of the first man—or even a direct act of creation for each human soul at some point between conception and birth. But man is no less a creation of God because he has emerged gradually within a world endowed by God with the potential for that emergence. So with regard to life after death. Whether we conceive of that life in terms of a divine act of recreation (either all together at the last day or individually at the moment of each person's death) or in terms of the survival of something inherent in man as he now is, God is the source of that life equally in both cases. It is not true that to speak of it in resurrection terms necessarily portrays its God-given character in a way that to speak of it in survival terms cannot. It does no more than shift the point at which the life-giving activity of God is described. It gives to the act of resurrection only what it has taken away from the initial act of creation. If man has an immortal soul, he has it only because God has so created him. It is not a matter of his own achievement. No 'Pelagian' derogation from the grace of God is involved. Nor should the kind of reasoning that I have been using be thought of as modern rationalization, glossing over a difference that was both evident to and intended by the early Fathers of the church. For them, as Wolfson puts it, 'both immortality and resurrection are volitional acts of God and not necessary acts of nature'.[2]

Similarly, we ought not to think that immortality necessarily implies an automatic and universal survival, while resurrection implies a conditional one for true believers only. The Apologists continually insist that the soul is not straightforwardly immortal in itself (whatever Plato may have said); it is potentially immortal; it lives by partaking in the life of God only because and so long as God wills.[3] While, from the other side, some of the Fathers when using the language of resurrection speak of Christ's resurrection necessarily effecting the resurrection of all men, believers and unbelievers alike, by virtue of his assumption of human nature in its totality.[4]

[2] H. A. Wolfson, 'Immortality and Resurrection in the Philosophy of the Church Fathers', in *Religious Philosophy*, Harvard University Press 1961, p.76.

[3] See e.g. Justin, *Dia. with Trypho* 6; Tatian, *Oratio* 13; Theophilus, *Ad Autolycum* 2,27; Irenaeus, *Adv. Haer.* 2,34,4.

[4] See e.g. Cyril Alex., *Comm. in John* x.10 (ed. Pusey II, 220–1).

At this point the argument is likely to take on a christological character. God, it may be replied, is certainly the
transcendent creator. But he is also redeemer, and some of
his purposes for mankind are only made known to us and
available for us through Christ. This, it may be claimed, is
the case with life after death. It is only through the resurrection of Christ that we have ground for believing in a life
after death and the possibility of participation in it. It is the
specifically christological character of Christian hope that
makes resurrection unquestionably the most appropriate
expression of our belief.

Here again the argument involves a number of points
which need to be distinguished. In the first instance, even
within Scripture itself the hope of resurrection, in the sense
of a personal life after death, does not begin with Jesus. It
emerges gradually in the later stages of the Old Testament
period and comes to expression more particularly through
the martyr experience of the Maccabean period, as witnessed,
for example, by the book of Daniel. The New Testament
makes it clear that the belief was held by the Pharisees at the
time of Jesus. Thus resurrection to a life beyond death was
not a totally new conception, wholly unknown before the
resurrection of Jesus himself, even though it may not have
been as firmly fixed an element in the Judaism of Jesus' day
as has sometimes been supposed. That his resurrection was
unexpected and miraculous for his contemporaries remains
true, for the expected resurrection was a general resurrection at the close of history. His was a resurrection before the
time. But it did not mark the introduction of a wholly new
conception.

Indeed, the existence of such beliefs before the resurrection of Jesus is not a matter of mere temporal priority. The
events following the death of Jesus were clearly of a varied

and puzzling nature. The records that we have speak of experiences of very differing kinds: the finding of the empty tomb, angelic appearances and messages, appearances of Jesus in differing forms not always equally recognizable and with varying degrees of physicality, visionary experiences such as that of Paul which in I Corinthians 15 he sets alongside other resurrection appearances to the disciples. Such varied phenomena were not immediately and obviously self-explanatory. They required interpretation, and they found that interpretation through the already existing category of resurrection. To misquote and misapply some familiar words of Paul: if there is no belief in the resurrection of the dead, then it cannot be believed that Christ was raised. The resurrection of Christ was not an event which was so self-evident that it had to be believed against all prior forms of expectation. The disciples' understanding of the aftermath of the death of Jesus in terms of resurrection was dependent upon the emergence of that concept within the Judaism of the immediately preceding centuries.

Contemporary belief in the resurrection of Jesus has a similar structure. Once we have abandoned the concept of Scripture as an external authority whose claims are to be accepted without challenge, we cannot evade our responsibility to adjudge and interpret even its most central affirmations. The resurrection of Jesus is not to be believed simply on the authority of the records. So strange a claim must be critically assessed. I have already indicated the perplexing variety of the evidence with which we have to deal. It is not possible here to enter upon a full discussion of it. The position which I wish to maintain is that our assessment of the evidence is bound (logically bound) to be related to our general expectations of what is conceivable. If there were nothing (literally nothing) in our more general experience that made the idea of a survival of death a conceivable notion, then we would be forced to conclude that in no sense could Jesus be understood to have survived death. Whether we felt able to provide any other explanation of the evidence that satisfied us or not, we would be forced to conclude that the so-called appearances must have been in this respect deceptive hallucinations. We can only adjudge them to be veridical in pointing to an overcoming of death on the part of Jesus, if on other grounds we believe such an eventuality possible. Thus the resurrection of Jesus in isolation cannot be treated as sole ground for Christian belief in life after death. It may be a necessary condition of such a belief; it cannot (unless combined with a wholly unacceptable understanding of scriptural authority) be a sufficient condition.

Thus an insistence that Christian hope of life after death is based on the resurrection of Christ does not allow us to evade the anthropological approach more readily associated with the idea of immortality. We have to pose the question: are there features of the human situation as such which point towards a belief in immortality for man? The evidence seems at first sight to indicate a strongly negative answer. All that we now know about the interrelation of the mental and the physical seems to make the conception of a personal life apart from its physical basis an unthinkable notion. To many this fact will seem to indicate a negative answer not only in the first instance but in the last instance as well. The case is a strong one, and those who judge in this way may be right. But a doubt remains. To any but a fully-fledged behaviourist, the nature of our personal existence, even though known only in relation to a physical nature, is sufficiently odd to give us pause. The mysterious character of personal being can be expressed in a variety of ways. It is not possible here to do more than to indicate that variety through phrases which different writers have used in their attempts to do justice to this basic characteristic of our human experience—such as 'the recessiveness of I' by which as subject I can stand back from and reflect upon myself as personal being or 'the self-transcendence' which is experienced in the making of 'free' moral decisions. To assess these intimations adequately would require the most careful analysis and profound reflection. I do not think they take us very far in establishing the likelihood of a life beyond death. I think they do point to a mysterious depth in personal existence which ought to restrain us from ruling out that possibility altogether. But it is important to remember their role in Christian belief as a whole. Even if it were true that God could and does give to men a life beyond death by a wholly new creative act of his own determination, it is difficult to see how we could know it to be true (assuming no explicit and absolutely authoritative revelation to be available to us) unless there were at least some indications of its plausibility in human experience as such. The *wholly* miraculous is the wholly incredible. What we believe about any particular thing cannot be totally incongruous with what we believe about all other particular things. If our belief is to be believable, some such anthropological substructure is essential. The indications, I suggest, are probably sufficient—but only just sufficient—for such a role.

We have been concerned so far with only one half of the christological form of argument. We have been considering the claim that Christ's resurrection is the sole ground for a belief in life after human death, and I have argued that it cannot fulfil that role without the independent support of intimations of immortality in human experience as a whole. We must now take up the other form of christological argument. It may be claimed that however varied the grounds for believing in the possibility of life after death, it is only through participation in the resurrection of Christ that man is able to realize that possibility. This claim is open to a narrower or wider interpretation. In its narrower form it would limit the enjoyment of life after death to those who with conscious faith have become believers in the Jesus who died and rose again in Palestine at the beginning of our era. I do not intend to discuss this form of the belief. It seems to me quite untenable, for reasons which will be familiar enough and which there is no need to develop here.

The other approach would give a less historical interpretation to 'participation in the resurrection of Christ'. It would see the phrase as including all those who have sought in this life to respond to those values which for the Christian are enbodied in the figure of Christ. In other words, it is a way of stressing that the life after death with which Christian faith is concerned is not simply a mere continuation of existence but that there is a qualitative aspect to it. Christian talk about 'eternal life' is not simply to be identified with talk about life after death. 'This is life eternal, to know thee, the only true God, and Jesus Christ whom thou hast sent.' Eternal life is something which can be said to characterize Christian experience here and now. This approach plays down the significance of physical death. The heart of the matter is a relationship between man and God which can be entered upon now and which death is simply unable to touch. When in the Johannine story Jesus responds to the incredulity of Martha, he deals first with the particular problem of Lazarus who has died: 'If a man has faith in me, even though he die he shall come to life'; he then puts the issue in a new and more basic perspective: 'No one who is alive, and has faith, shall ever die.' A faith relationship with

God through Christ unites a man to the ultimate source of life in a way which death is powerless to destroy.

Such an approach does not necessarily involve the concept of resurrection. What I have called the new and more basic perspective moves away from the idea of resurrection from death and speaks of the man of faith simply not dying. It would fit admirably with an understanding of immortality like that of the Apologists to which I referred earlier. Nevertheless, there is an important link between this approach and the language of resurrection. The point may be made in a general way something like this. What God gives to man in the order of creation is the potentialities of his nature and of his situation, something that he has, whatever use he makes or fails to make of them. What man makes of those potentialities in response to his environment (and, therefore, whether he recognizes it or not, in response to God) corresponds to what has been traditionally described as God's gifts in the order of redemption. This distinction, it may I think be argued, is formal rather than actual, since we never merely exist; we always exist in some determinate form to which we have ourselves contributed. Nevertheless, if we were concerned with the bare fact of continued existence after death, the language of immortality understood as a gift of God in the order of creation would be fully appropriate. But if we are concerned at the same time with the quality of life, as Christian faith emphatically is, resurrection language is more suitable. It is readily at home in both contexts. It can refer quite simply to continued existence after death. But it can also be used metaphorically of the transition to that new quality of life which is called 'eternal'. In Pauline language, resurrection to newness of life is the experience of every Christian. The appropriateness of the term to express this second concept is to be seen not only in the dependence of such experience for the Christian on the fact of Christ's conquest of death. It is to be seen also in the fact that an element of negation, which psychological and spiritual writers alike find it natural to speak of as a kind of dying, is an essential feature of the way to such life.

The use of the one term 'resurrection' is of special value, therefore, in pointing to the integration of these two themes in Christian thought. Yet the implication of that integration may be understood in diametrically opposed ways. To some people it carries the suggestion that the qualitative sense is the only proper sense. Just as most Christians today would see ancient belief in the resuscitation of the flesh as false if taken literally, but true if treated as a symbol of personal survival, so it is clearly possible to regard belief in personal survival as false if taken literally, but true if treated as a symbol of the possibility of rising to a truer and fuller life now. But though clearly a possible move to make, it is equally clearly not a necessary one. The integration of the two themes can be seen very differently, as fully consistent with belief in a God who is both 'life' and 'love'. Seeing it in this way tends rather to confirm than to deny belief in personal survival of death.

Arguments from what is consistent with the believed character of God are dangerously speculative in character; yet they are perhaps the only proper form of theological argument open to us. God has created a world whose purpose incorporates, though it may not be bounded by, the emergence and the development of personal beings. Knowledge of God and the possibility of loving response to him is open to them; it is not forced upon them, but nothing is of greater importance or significance for life. The original emergence of a hope of life after death in the Old Testament tradition derived from a conviction of the fundamental moral injustice of a world of God's creation in which such a faithful response to God might entail nothing but misery and brutal death. If couched in purely moral terms, the argument is highly unsatisfactory. But in religious discourse, moral terms always point beyond themselves to the more ultimate realm of the personal and the spiritual. In the answer of Jesus to the Sadducees' question, it is not merely justice but the inviolability of a loving covenant relationship which ensures that Abraham, Isaac and Jacob must still live to God. The nub of the argument is the inconceivability of God entering into such a relationship with the saints of old, and yet allowing it to be simply expunged by death. The whole tenor of the gospel as a revelation of God in Jesus Christ points to a God whose love knows no limits to which it will not go in eliciting and establishing such a response of love. There does seem to be a fundamental inconsistency in the conception of a God whose purpose in creation includes as so prominent a feature the emergence of personal life capable of response to him, but whose purpose also allows for the utter extinction of those relationships of love, developed so gradually, so profoundly and yet with such tantalizing incompleteness.

So far we have been concerned with the contrast between resurrection and immortality. Resurrection certainly appears to be the richer symbol of the two religiously, primarily because of the way in which the associations which the term has acquired in history link together the ideas of the overcoming of evil and the overcoming of death. Apart from that, I do not think that it says anything which could not be expressed equally adequately in terms of immortality. But we must now turn our attention more specifically to the second half of the traditional credal phrase: 'resurrec-

tion of the *body*'. It was no accident that the church chose
to express itself in this way. It was the form in which, as
we have already seen, the hope of a future life first emerged
within Judaism. The Hebrew understanding of man as a
psycho-somatic unity made it the most natural form in
which to express the concept of a future life which was to
be something more than a pale shadow of the present.
Moreover, the resurrection of Jesus was recorded as taking
a bodily form. But the idea was emphasized in the church
not merely because of its origins, but because of the role it
fulfilled in Christian thought as a whole. Three things in
particular it was felt to emphasize. In the first place, it
stressed the completeness of life after death. It was not
normally felt to be in conflict with the idea of the immortality of the soul; it was felt rather to add to it. Secondly, it
underlined the real continuity between this life and the life
to come; it depicted the identity of the one who had lived his
life here and the one who received the fruits of 'his conduct
in the body' in the after life. Thirdly, it was valued as giving
clear expression, in contrast to Gnosticism, to a positive evaluation of this life and of the material world. It showed that
matter was not the outcome of sin or in necessary conflict
with the divine; rather it was something good, ultimately
to be taken up into the fulfilment of the divine purpose.

If belief in the resurrection of the body is still to be
affirmed, in what sense can it be understood today? And
can it, in any sense open to us today, continue to fulfil the
kind of role that it has fulfilled in the past?

The resurrection of Jesus is far less relevant than might at
first sight appear. The differing degrees of physicality implied
are one of the puzzling features of the records. But that is
not the essential factor which makes the resurrection of
Jesus irrelevant to the nature of our resurrection in

this regard. It seems clear that the bodily aspect of the resurrection stories is directly linked to communication with the still living disciples. In other words, its context is in relation to the physical existence of the disciples. It cannot be extrapolated from that context and used as evidence for the nature of resurrection life itself.

What we have to ask, therefore, is whether in the context of a contemporary understanding of man the concept can still properly fulfil those three aims for which it was valued in the early church. Certainly it is for reasons of the same kind that it tends to be welcomed by contemporary theologians. Modern scientific knowledge makes clear that man is a psycho-somatic unity, that his body is much more than the physical envelope of a non-physical entity. This is not infrequently claimed as so close a parallel to the Hebrew conception of man that it provides without further ado clear justification of the appropriateness of continuing to speak in the same terms of a 'resurrection of the body'. But caution is called for. Even if both pictures share a non-dualistic character, they are not thereby to be regarded as identical. Nevertheless, it is true that it is not merely over-hasty identification but also careful philosophical reflection that has pointed in this direction. A body of some kind, it is argued, is essential to the expression of a self. A bodiless form of existence is either strictly inconceivable or, if conceivable at all, wholly undesirable. Thus John Baillie speaks of it as something 'most of us will shrink' from 'no less than did St Paul',[5] and John Macquarrie describes it as 'a shadowy kind of sub-existence' that 'might well turn out to be intolerably boring and frustrating'.[6] Lloyd Geering uses even

[5] John Baillie, *And the Life Everlasting*, Oxford University Press 1934, p.254.

[6] John Macquarrie, *Principles of Christian Theology*, SCM Press 1966, p.324.

stronger language: 'The thought,' he writes, 'of being eternally conscious, yet without body, should such a state be even conceivable any more, must be the very worst kind of hell that one could imagine.'[7] And finally Professor Strawson ends the chapter on 'Persons' in his book *Individuals* with the words: 'Disembodied survival, on such terms as these, may well seem unattractive. No doubt it is for this reason that the orthodox have wisely insisted on the resurrection of the body.'[8] Now the theologian should certainly pay heed to what responsible philosophers say, but he is not so impoverished that he must be grateful for every crumb of comfort that falls from the philosopher's table. Despite the frequent repetition and wide acceptance of this line of reasoning, I am not convinced of its soundness. God is bodiless and inconceivable; but this is not (in Christian eyes at least) ground for denying his existence or regretting its form. Moreover, it is eternal life, life in relation to that God, of which the Christian is trying to speak in all his talk about life after death. The whole subject is one of which it is difficult to speak at all; it is certainly not clear to me (in view of Christian belief about God) that to speak of life after death in terms of a body makes such speech either more intelligible or more attractive.

Let us then consider the other two functions that 'resurrection of the body' language is designed to fulfil. The second was the concept of continuity. Certainly one may find in much philosophical writing the idea that the body, rather than something non-physical such as memory, is the focus of personal continuity. Can this then be applied to the transition of death? Some people certainly make the

[7] Lloyd Geering, *Resurrection—A Symbol of Hope*, Hodder and Stoughton 1971, p.213.

[8] P. F. Strawson, *Individuals*, Methuen 1964, p.116.

attempt. Arthur Peacocke, in giving reasons for preferring resurrection to immortality, says: 'The resurrected human personality is continuous with the living human personality, including his molecular, material aspect, and is derived out of it without loss of individuality.'[9] Peter Geach appears to believe that personal survival necessarily involves 'that from a human corpse there will arise at some future date a new human body, continuous in some way with the corpse'.[10] This he seems to regard as possible, though I am bound to say that even allowing for the qualifying 'in some way', it is just about the one thing that seems to me to be clearly impossible. Whatever may be meant by a resurrection body, it is, I believe, inconceivable that it should have any kind of physical continuity with the body we now have. Thus the concept of the resurrection of the body, even if it should have a use as expressing a fullness of existence after death (which I have questioned), cannot with any appropriateness whatever give expression to the idea of a continuity of existence with our present life. For however that continuity is conveyed, it is precisely *not* conveyed through the body.

For essentially similar reasons, the concept does not seem to me well suited to express its third traditional function— a positive attitude to the physical aspect of our present life. If a resurrection body is neither a part of nor derived from the stuff of this physical universe, then it is hardly a natural symbol of the positive significance of physicality in the purposes of God.

In this second half of the paper I have been concentrating attention on the second half of the phrase 'resurrection of the *body*', with an implicit contrast between body and soul.

[9] A. R. Peacocke, *Science and the Christian Experiment*, Oxford University Press 1971, p.168.
[10] Peter Geach, *God and the Soul*, Routledge 1969, p.28.

Much recent philosophical discussion, as I have indicated, has stressed the value of the traditional belief at precisely this point. In that discussion it has been strongly argued that if life after death is a possible concept at all, it must incorporate some form of belief in the resurrection of the body. For how else could individual identification, mutual recognition and personal agency—all integral to our understanding of personal existence—be possible at all? The problems that such considerations raise are real and have to be taken seriously. Nonetheless, having tried to weigh those considerations carefully, I do not for myself find any advantage in the traditional term. 'Body' language does not seem to me to be well suited to express those things for which it was valued in the early days of the church. Despite the claim that it makes life after death more conceivable and more attractive, it seems to me to be of very doubtful value and perhaps even rather dangerous.

Dangerous in two ways. Arguments that stress the necessity of some kind of body for the expression of a self and for any form of communication with other selves are very closely related to those arguments which show the body to be the essential focus of continuity in personal life. I am not convinced that one can have the first without the second. And if so, it means that just in so far as they show resurrection of the body to be the only conceivable, or at least the only worthwhile, form of a belief in life after death, they also serve to show that it is not a possible belief for us to hold.

But they are dangerous also in a more fundamental sense that lies behind this particular difficulty. The underlying problem about believing in life after death is the problem of meaning—not just the relative adequacy or inadequacy of traditional pictures of feasting, music, rest or perpetual worship, but the problem of convincing ourselves when we reflect on such questions as continuing identity and the possibility of personal existence without the physical basis of personality that the concept has any meaning at all. Now the attempt to deal with this basic problem in terms of a sophisticated understanding of the resurrection of the body tends to suggest that in order to convince ourselves that the concept has meaning, we ought to be able at least in principle to envisage what it is that we are believing. I am sufficient of an empiricist to feel the force of this, but I am not convinced by it. It is not true of our belief in God. There we need to have pointers in our experience which justify our speaking about the transcendent; but once we have committed ourselves to speaking of the transcendent we have to acknowledge (for both logical and religious reasons) our inability to envisage that of which we are speaking. So also with life after death. This is fundamentally a corollary of our faith in God. If, as I have tentatively argued, there are in this case, too, sufficient pointers to justify our making the assertion, we need not necessarily be over-concerned at our inability to envisage that which we are led to affirm. That is, rather, what we ought to expect.

If I am right here (and I recognize that that is a very big 'if'), a good deal of recent writing on the resurrection of the body as expressive of the continuation of individual personal life is misconceived. This leads me to make a final and extremely tentative suggestion. I hinted at the beginning that to concentrate on the problem of individual survival of death represented a shift of emphasis from the early Christian tradition and might involve an element of distortion. The concept of the resurrection of the body has a corporate as well as a corporeal dimension—the two being intertwined in the concept of the body of Christ. There is much in the Christian tradition as a whole that points in that direction. To take but one example from the teaching of Jesus himself. When it is said that those who attain to the resurrection of the dead neither marry nor are given in marriage but are like the angels, this implies not merely that they are no longer physical beings but that the profound union of love which in this life characterizes exclusively the relationship with one another in marriage is in the life to come characteristic of all relationships within the communion of saints. It is not a falling back into a more individualistic way of life than we now experience, but a passing beyond it into newer and richer kinds of relationship. So, too, with a more general study of human nature. This brings out not only the dependence of what we are as persons on our physical nature, but also its dependence on our relations with other persons. It is a healthy development when men find their life enlarged through marriage or through participation in some social grouping. The isolation that may come to people through bereavement or through exclusion from such a social group is felt to be an impoverishment of their own being, a kind of death.

Now none of these lines of thought suggest the total elimination of the person. They envisage, rather, the enhancement of the personal through a fuller union with other persons. Nevertheless, it is not perhaps illegitimate to ask whether there may not be pointers here to a conception of the divine purpose in which human life is not simply negated, but in which the individuality of personal being is transcended.

Such a suggestion has obvious difficulties. First and most obviously, is it intelligible? Does it in fact mean anything? Possibly not. But I have already argued that the conceivability criterion cannot be rigorously applied in this area.

I am not sure that my suggestion is any worse off on that score than the traditional more individual view. Just as personal life itself emerges out of more primitive forms of biological existence and cannot be described or imagined in terms limited to those more primitive forms, it does not seem impossible that individual personal existence might be transcended in the consummation of God's purpose in a manner which would be a fulfilment rather than a negation of our present existence.

A second objection might be put in this way. You have argued, it might be said, that belief in a personal life after death has its main ground in the character of a God who is the friend of Abraham, who enters into personal relationships with his children; does this not imply that if there is survival of death at all, it must be of an individual and personal kind? Certainly the concept of God entering into personal relationships with each of his children is a fundamental Christian concept. But it is an imperfect manner of speech. Treated as direct description it involves a falsely anthropomorphic conception of God. There is more to the being of God than is conveyed by speaking of him as 'a person'. May there not, then, be more to the consummation of man's relationship to God than that of an individual personal relationship?

But speculation has already been allowed to take us too far. What I have tried to argue is that the Christian hope of life after death may not, despite all the obvious difficulties, be an unreasonable belief, if it is closely integrated with belief in God. I have argued that we are equally unable to imagine it, whether we attempt to do so in terms of a disembodied soul-substance, of a spiritual body or as some more fully corporate form of existence, but that this is not necessarily a fatal objection to the belief. I have also argued that there is much less difference between the two formulations in terms of resurrection of the body and immortality of the soul than is usually claimed. I have suggested that there is advantage from a Christian point of view in resurrection language, but I have expressed serious doubts about the advantages often claimed for body language in this context. All such language has, of course, to be seen as extremely indirect symbolic language and not as description of what will be. 'Brethren, we are the children of God; it does not yet appear what we shall be.' The Christian, even or rather especially the Christian theologian, should not be ashamed to express a like agnosticism.

INDEX OF NAMES

INDEX OF SUBJECTS